In Memory of my husband, Father Peter Dally

May 14, 1928 – July 6, 2007

Father Peter and Mary Vincent Dally
Tulsa, Oklahoma
1997

Acknowledgements

"Catholic Priest and Husband" has been a work in progress for more than twenty years. When I first began, I thought I had a personal story to tell. As the months and years passed I realized that the story is never-ending for it is not just our story but the story of nearly one hundred married couples in the Pastoral Provision.

I cannot begin to thank the countless folks who walked beside me through the years of ministry, and who gave me assistance and encouragement with this book. I would like to thank my writers group in Olympia, Washington - good and faithful friends. I joined the biography writers at Southwestern Oregon Community College in Coos Bay in 2009 when I moved to the Oregon Coast after Father Peter's death. I thank them all, particularly Sally Harrold for her leadership and expertise. It is with their encouragement that I finished the book.

My readers were invaluable. They include Mary Sherman, the wife of the late Father Gary Sherman, Mother Anastasia of Holy Theophany Byzantine Monastery, Richard Perry, Rosalie Lupcho,

Dr. Rudy and Mavis Wolf, Sally Harrold, Elaine Dunham, and Don Hanisch. Georgianna Ricketts was an invaluable resource in the sharing of my stories of the Osage Native American communities of Skiatook and Hominy, Oklahoma.

I would like to thank the many Catholics of Oklahoma for their support and encouragement for our ministry and my writing. They made it all possible! Not least, I am grateful for the support of my late husband, Father Peter who cheered me on when I simply wanted to give up.

This book is a true story. Incidents and conversations are written from memory and notes, and are meant to capture the spirit of my unique experience from my point of view. Some readers will not agree with my personal perspective. I ask only that you consider that these are my *personal* experiences and impressions. The story timeline is in general chronological order in an effort to group like incidents together for clarity.

The term "Okie" is used as a term of endearment for the people we shared our lives with for eighteen years in Oklahoma. The definitions in the glossary are taken from "The Catholic Encyclopedia", Copyright 1976 by Robert C. Broderick, published by Our Sunday Visitor, and from the Pastoral Provision documents.

Mary Vincent Dally
August 22, 2013

"Do we have no right to take along a Christian wife,
as do also the rest of the apostles,
and the brothers of the Lord, and Peter?"

1 Corinthians 9:5
Catholic Study Bible

-1-

June 1985

Tulsa, Oklahoma

"He says he doesn't need me anymore," Peter said as we drove home. He had just finished celebrating his second Sunday-evening Mass at Holy Family Cathedral.

"Who said that?" I asked.

"Well, the Pastor, of course."

"I don't understand. He doesn't need you?"

"He says he has another priest coming in. He says he will send me a check for the last two Sundays."

"That's going against Bishop Beltran. He can't do that, can he?"

"Well, the point is, he did it."

"What will you do? And he shouldn't be paying you anyway. The Diocese gives you a stipend."

"I'll see the Bishop when he gets back from his vacation. He'll handle it. It's not up to me." Peter sighed, turned to me, and reached for my hand. "I'm sorry to put you through yet another crisis. But you have to realize, I don't want to be there if the pastor doesn't want me."

I fumbled in my purse for a tissue. I looked out the window as we passed the mansions on Twenty-first Street and thought of the struggles of the past five years, of all that we had given up for this ministry. I turned to him and said, "You *are* a Catholic priest and no matter what they do, they can't take that away."

"I wonder."

Throughout the application and acceptance process, other priests and their wives in the Pastoral Provision, had told us not to worry, that once Peter was ordained, other Catholic priests would accept him. We were a part of the Holy Father's own program, they assured us, and, whether celibate or married, Catholics honor the gift of priesthood for its own sake. It is not a deserved sacrament, but a man's response to a call from God and affirmed by the Church at ordination.

The priests' assignments were appointments made by the bishop of the diocese. The letter Peter received from Bishop Beltran before his ordination outlined his multiple assignments:

Masses and confessions at Holy Family Cathedral;

Mass and pastoral care at St. John Medical Center two days a week;

Mass two days a week for the Christian Brothers at Bishop Kelley High School;

Pastoral care of Catholic patients at Hillcrest Hospital and Tulsa Regional Medical Center.

The priests and brothers to whom Peter was assigned received a copy of the letter as well. Yet the pastor of the cathedral ignored Bishop Beltran's directive. I could not comprehend his behavior, and I questioned what, if anything, would happen when our bishop returned. He led and most of the priests followed, but realistically I did not think it likely that the bishop would stand up against a priest who was a leader in the diocese, and privately, I wondered if there would be another weekend assignment for Peter.

Two days later while we were eating dinner, the phone rang.

"That was one of the Christian Brothers. They would like to continue with the priest who has been saying Mass for them. They don't need me." Returning to his meal, he smiled. "That's two more mornings free."

"What's going on with these guys?" I asked.

"Bishop will take care of it."

I started to return dishes to the kitchen, then stopped and turned to face him. "But Bishop told us from the beginning that you should expect to say Mass for a parish or monastery every day."

"Yes...."

"Why would they ordain you if they're not going to use you?"

"I don't know. I have no idea how they think, Mary."

"These are the same priests who ordained you, laid their hands on you only two weeks ago. I can't believe this is happening."

"Bishop Beltran will handle it."

While we waited for the Bishop to return from his vacation, Peter carried out his hospital assignments. All three hospitals were large and served eastern Oklahoma, as well as adjacent states with their specialties. Yet, situated in the heart of the Bible belt, Oklahoma Catholics numbered about four percent of the population. His work at these hospitals filled only two mornings a week. Peter appeared to ignore what seemed to be a real bias against him as he set about making use of the unexpected free time. I think that he was so amazed that he had actually been ordained a Catholic priest in spite of being married and a former Protestant that he didn't strongly question the reason for the pattern that was emerging.

As for me, I thought only of the unfairness of it all as I allowed the situation to eat away at me. For what had we sacrificed so much? For what had we moved more than 2,000 miles from our children? Would these senseless games never end? In a kind of limbo, I feared that we would remain outsiders in this diocese we had hoped to call our home. Then I reminded myself that fear is the absence of faith. I had known our ministry in the Catholic Church would not be easy. I just didn't expect it to be so hard.

When Bishop Beltran returned, Peter met with him in his office.

"Those were *my* appointments. A priest cannot dismiss you, Father Peter. I am the only person who can change your assignment." His face reddened as he spoke.

And later in the meeting he asked, "How does that make you feel?"

"I'm disappointed, but I can't force him to want me there."

As weeks became months, the sweltering summer heat gave way to autumn's beauty and milder weather but we did not hear further from Bishop Beltran regarding Peter's assignments.

As we walked to the hospital one day, I said, "It doesn't look as though the Bishop is going to do anything for you."

"Seems that way."

"Why would he ignore this insult to his leadership?"

"You have to realize that he depends on the good will of his priests for the success of the diocese," Peter said.

"But he *is* the bishop."

"What's he going to do if his priests won't work with him?"

Still, disappointed in our bishop's inaction, the cloud of gloom hung over me, coloring my world with anxiety and apprehension. I would not talk to friends about it and I could not change anything. We were virtually helpless and at the mercy of those clerics who held control over our lives. I wondered if others around us realized what was happening; it did seem to me that to shun a brother priest was a contradiction of the vows each of them had made. Peter continued to have faith that Bishop Beltran would remedy the situation when the time was right, and he found peace in that belief.

However, I felt alone and the aloneness overwhelmed me. We quietly drifted apart as more and more, I became reluctant to share my concerns with Peter. I wondered if I should start to plan for our return to the Washington. Sometimes it seemed that I was more concerned than Peter as he patiently appeared to accept our fate. In this "dark night of the soul," I prayed with small faith for the grace of acceptance for Peter and his priesthood, and for our life together. I asked God to lighten the darkness that encircled me, for it seemed to me that we could not remain in Tulsa as our situation appeared now. I stuffed all this down inside me, going through the motions of each day as best I knew how, not seeing, or savoring the beauty around me.

However, just to survive is hardly a life or a ministry. The culture of the Catholic Church was entirely different from that which we had experienced for twenty-eight years in the Episcopal Church. The unwritten customs and civilities of the past were no more, and there now seemed to be a code of behavior to which we converts were not privy. I reminded myself that God provides all of our needs and in His providence, His plan was unfolding, not as we wished but in His way. Could it be that He had something better in store for us than we could imagine now? Surely, the Holy Spirit would bless Peter's priesthood and our life together in this new ministry, however conflicted or distressing the journey seems now.

-2-

Several months before Peter's ordination the superior of the Sisters of the Sorrowful Mother who operated St. John Medical Center called to offer me a position as her personal secretary. I already had a good job with Impact Systems, a small training organization in Tulsa. I liked it there and felt reluctant to leave, but the invitation felt like a victory of sorts and seemed to promise the acceptance and normalcy I longed for in the Catholic Church.

I took the job without a face-to-face interview. When I offered my resignation to Nicki Bjornsen, owner of Impact Systems, I wept.

When I told my friend, Mary Sherman, she said, "You're crying? If this is what you really want, you should be happy; not crying."

Ignoring her insight, I said, "Oh, I think it's just my emotions. I really want to work for the Church."

Two weeks later I began the new job.

Each day I drove to the convent in Broken Arrow. I soon found some peace in the friendships I made with the sisters, especially those who were retired.

However, even there I could not escape ecclesiastical politics. I realized my total naiveté when I learned that some sisters had close personal friendships with priests. Unexpectedly some seemed to compare their friendships with my marriage to a priest. It was distressing for me, a woman married for twenty-eight years with grown children. I felt saddened and self-conscious that normal relationships with the opposite sex, even close friendships, were not acceptable behavior for priests and religious in the Catholic Church.

At this time in my life, I attended daily Mass and went to the sisters' chapel before my workday began. However, after Peter's ordination, I wanted to be with him as often as I could when he celebrated Mass. The retired nuns, with nothing more to do than engage in prayer and meditation—and a little benign gossip—observed everything I did and soon noticed that I no longer attended their Mass on a regular basis. One sister hinted that she wondered why I no longer came.

"I really want to be with Peter when he celebrates Mass," I explained.

Her clear blue eyes twinkled. "I understand, dear," she said.

Later when the same sister mentioned it again, I confided to her, "Peter frequently celebrates Mass at home and I am his only witness."

"Oh?"

Embarrassed, I said, "I'm afraid that the assignments Bishop Beltran made for him have not been honored by some. He has no week-end Mass assignment and two of his week-day Masses have been cancelled."

Tears came to her eyes and she said simply, "Bishop Beltran should have stood his ground."

In this environment I did not feel scrutinized and judged as I so often experienced with some priests and sisters, but only supported and strengthened. Still, something was going wrong in my life. My attempt to become and feel more a part of the life of the Catholic Church had not eased the sadness that haunted me. I realized that I was not happy working for Sister. The migraine headaches that had afflicted me for years had worsened; the debilitating pain was more frequent, more severe, and nearly always lasted several days.

"My job isn't what I thought it would be," I said to Peter one evening while we were eating dinner. "I think I'm getting a little paranoid." I laughed.

"I was afraid this wasn't going to work out."

"Since I didn't interview with Sister, I guess I have no one to blame but myself."

"What's happening?"

"In the past, I've held complex positions with a lot of responsibility. I've been a trusted employee and expected to handle confidential information. Do you know I am not allowed in her office alone? She keeps her roll-top desk locked and she even locks her office door when she goes to the restroom."

"I've always heard that nuns and monks are secretive."

"But I'm her assistant."

"I doubt that it has anything to do with you or your job."

"I don't think she trusts me."

"She probably doesn't trust anybody. I doubt that she locks up because of you."

"Another thing, I don't have enough to do and she doesn't want me to find tasks to keep busy."

"Just don't let it get to you. Go there. Do your job and just accept Sister for who she is. I'm sure it's not personal."

"I know you must be right."

"Don't let her actions determine how you think and behave."

"Okay." I dropped the subject and, feeling that to leave the position would be a failure on my part, I resolved to finish out the year.

On days when Sister was out of the office and my work done, faced with another migraine, I would go into the file room where it was dark and lie face down on the carpet just to feel the soothing coolness against my face. However, nothing helped. My life spiraled into an ever-deepening cavern of pain.

Outside of my work and Peter's ministry, my closest friend was Mary Sherman, the wife of a former Lutheran pastor who had been ordained a Catholic priest with Peter. We had lunch together on the first Friday of each month. Even though we numbered only two, we called these lunches the priests' wives meeting.

I remember on a Friday not too long after our husbands' ordination, Mary quipped, "Well, they're ordained. What'll we do now?"

"You could have another baby," I said with a smile, knowing that my biological clock had stopped ticking while hers had not. We both laughed. Ten months later Mary gave birth to Joshua.

-3-

As weeks became months, it appeared that Bishop Beltran had made no effort to reinstate Peter's assignments.

Still, there was so much bitter sweetness in Peter's new priesthood. After five years of preparation with all of the expectations, disappointments and occasional victories, we continued to hope that we could successfully enter into the life and ministry of the Roman Catholic Church. To this end, we fretted over the uncertainties of identifying courtesies and appropriate behaviors in this new environment that we found to be far different from our experiences in the Episcopal Church's ministry. We had moved from a tradition where priests' wives are revered and cherished, into the Roman Catholic experience where, without exception in the U.S., priests do not marry. We found that in public settings, priests and sisters were sometimes embarrassed, not knowing how to begin or what to say about the presence of a priest's wife. In all of our years in the Catholic Church, many failed to realize that the best and by far the easiest solution was a simple explanation of the Pastoral Provision and the exception to celibacy for former Protestant ministers that rightly honors both the priesthood and Christian marriage.

We were perplexed as simple everyday occurrences like going to church services and dinners became complicated. For example, if my name was not on the invitation, did it mean that I was not invited, or was I simply overlooked? I think our friends and colleagues most often understood our uncertainties and the awkwardness of the situation. We tried to get the word around that we would assume I was not included if my name didn't appear on the invitation. Peter often picked up the phone and called to find out. We found this relaxed way of handling it easily accepted by others, especially laypersons.

As I talked with other couples in the Pastoral Provision, we all agreed that although our roles as Catholic priests and wives were more complex in many ways, many aspects of our faith lives were easier now than in the Episcopal Church. Without the pressures of whether we were high church or low church or catholic or protestant, we were now free to live the Catholic faith that we loved and which was the heart of our conversion to Roman Catholicism. However, at the same time, the Catholic clerical hierarchy was not prepared to include priests with wives and families in the ordinary life of the Church and this made our day-to-day ministries more difficult.

Naïve as we were, Peter and I did not have the slightest inkling of the disquiet a priest with a wife would create in the Catholic Church. I remember Bishop Beltran's often-repeated comment: "You have no idea how unusual this is." I can only assume that this is why the assimilation process was awkward and sometimes embarrassing, and required a lot of creative thinking, not to mention charity, for them and for us.

I think Bishop Beltran was better prepared than most bishops I knew of, but it soon became clear that even in the Diocese of Tulsa, they did not understand all that was needed to assimilate the married priests and their families. How could men who had been Catholic all their lives know the Protestant tradition from which we came? Why would they know it was necessary or helpful to be aware of our backgrounds, so different from theirs? Moreover, to be fair, we knew relatively little about their journey. Both sides needed education and sensitivity.

On the other hand, Bishop Beltran and chancery officials had generously prepared for the material needs of the priests' families. We were surprised because we had been told by others in the Pastoral Provision not to expect monetary compensation of any kind. In the Diocese of Tulsa, we experienced remarkable sensitivity with regard to our needs. Bishop Beltran and the personnel board provided housing, household furnishings, and stipends for the three married priest candidates from the day we arrived in the Diocese. When the men were ordained, the Diocese purchased term life insurance for each of them. In short, our material needs were thoughtfully and generously met.

We found that it made little difference to laypersons whether a priest was married or celibate. They appreciated Peter's attention to pastoral care and his love for the Eucharist as well as other tenets of the faith that he openly cherished.

One person wrote to me, "It seems so natural to me to see you beside Father Peter, sharing his ministry and touching our lives, bringing family depth to our faith journeys."

Another wrote, "What a difference there is in confessing heartbreaks and pains that flow within a family to a priest who is both husband and father."

Many laypersons said that if the Pastoral Provision was the Holy Father's, of course they were behind it. However, some priests and sisters were openly opposed to the program. They thought a married man undeserving of the gift and, particularly, the status of priesthood, of which they seemed to say that celibacy was the primary condition. Could they not see that whether celibate or married, the priesthood is imbued with the sacramental grace of apostolic succession? When laypersons suggested that their objections sprang from jealousy, I did not believe it, but I have come to realize that envy did exist at times.

Some objected because they feared the Vatican was setting a precedent aimed toward ordaining married men, rather than women, which they favored as a more acceptable direction for the Church. Unquestionably, their reactions resulted from a complex variety of sources and issues.

We became aware that spiritual formation is important in the Catholic priesthood. Among the priest candidates and newly ordained, each man's spirituality and faith practice is influenced and formed by those priests with whom he associates. Individuality and creative thinking are discouraged. The ability to fit in is so important, that an out of the ordinary candidate may be counseled, even pressured, to drop out.

Having brought along the unusual baggage of wives and children, and without any serious program of formation it was not realistic to expect the married priests to fit in. However, throughout the initial application process and after ordination, the necessity to "fit in" seemed a recurring theme and, for us, felt like a critical requirement for acceptance by other priests.

I can't say that we had not been warned. I remember our pastor at St. John Vianney Church on Vashon Island saying, "Peter, you don't need to be a Catholic priest to validate your ministry. Stay where you are. You will never fit in."

Others said the same thing.

A layman, who had been a Franciscan seminarian, married and father of two said, "They will never accept you."

"Why?" we asked.

"Because you didn't go to seminary with them. You will never fit in."

I laughed. "How could going to seminary with them possibly make a difference?"

Nevertheless, it did make a difference. It should have been a warning and indeed, I think it was meant to be, but we did not recognize it and I doubt that it would have made any difference if we had. We simply felt that the opportunity had presented itself and Peter was called to be a Catholic priest with me beside him. To us, that was more important for the church than the obscurity of 'fitting in'.

Without a formation program for the married priests and their wives, we repeatedly stumbled, fell, and picked ourselves up. We felt an unmistakable sense of living in the borderlands of our new life in the Catholic Church. More than anything, we felt frustrated that we had no answer about why the priests and brothers had not honored Peter's assignments. Bishop Beltran's silence continued with no indication that the situation would change.

Then one morning in late fall, Peter received a telephone call from one of the Christian Brothers. He hung up and turned to me. "They want me to celebrate Mass for them on Wednesday mornings."

"I heard. I guess you're going to," I said.

"Of course. I'll do whatever they want."

I felt a twinge of bitterness, but I was proud of Peter's willingness to accept the situation.

Soon, the superior of the Sisters of the Sorrowful Mother, for whom I worked, called him. "Father Peter, would you be able to celebrate Mass on Tuesday mornings for the infirm sisters at our St. Clare Convent?"

"Yes."

"We pay a stipend and mileage."

"That's not necessary. I receive a stipend from the Diocese."

"It's our policy. We would not want you to come at your own expense."

We had not expected that he would be paid extra in addition to his regular monthly diocesan priest's stipend. Still, with three children in college, we appreciated the sisters' generosity.

It did not dampen his enthusiasm when other priests told Peter that saying Mass for infirm sisters fell to elderly or less favored priests. The sisters inspired Peter and he felt privileged to be with them.

When it was time for the Mass, they came in wheelchairs or with the aid of walkers, moving slowly down the long halls of the convent nursing home, often dressed in robes and slippers. Only three of them wore habits and monastic veils. As I watched them move slowly toward the chapel with determination and purpose, I saw women on their way to work. Even in the last stages of their lives, these holy women continued in their dedication. One had only to enter the door of their chapel to know that theirs was a powerhouse of prayer.

Their community was founded on the principles of Franciscan spirituality. During the months that he was with them, Peter wrote an icon of the San Damiano Crucifix, the cross of St. Francis of Assisi. It hangs at the back of their chapel.

Within a few weeks the Prioress at St. Joseph Benedictine Monastery in Tulsa telephoned. "Father Peter, can you help us out this Sunday? Our chaplain has to assist in one of the parishes."

I wondered why the monastery chaplain had to assist in a parish when there was a priest, Peter, already free who could help. Peter didn't question it. He was simply happy to serve the Benedictine sisters.

"Yes. I'll be glad to."

"Stay and share brunch with us, and bring Mary."

"Thank you, Sister. I will."

Soon the Prioress called him nearly every week to celebrate the Sunday Mass. We felt at home with the sisters as we visited with them in their dining room over brunch after each Eucharist. Since their chaplain was usually gone on Sundays and Peter was available, he became their permanent substitute. So began a period in which we were with them nearly every Sunday.

While we had not heard from Bishop Beltran, we saw his hand in the request to say Mass for the Christian Brothers, as well as in the invitations from both communities of sisters. Moreover, the pastor who had dismissed Peter after two Sundays had begun to call him to fill in for his associate who was frequently unable to celebrate Mass. Peter went, his demeanor without a hint of bitterness.

While it might seem that Peter had been relegated to the leftovers as far as priestly duties were concerned, the Holy Spirit was at work in other ways in my life. I soon realized that the Benedictine liturgies were exactly what I needed. The sisters' serenity and their simple singing of the ancient chants and hymns were similar to the liturgies in the Episcopal Church. I felt at home and not so far removed from the peace and beauty of the Anglican worship I had left behind when we became Catholics. Although Catholic Mass was beautiful it did not contain the grace and poetry of the prose I had loved in the Episcopal Church's Book of Common Prayer.

Sunday brunch was a heartwarming experience as well. Their sense of humor and their non-critical companionship strengthened and reassured us of our rightful place in their lives.

Our time with the Sisters served as a kind of respite from the stress and uncertainty that had clouded our days in the years since 1980 when Peter first learned of the Pastoral Provision. Our lives began a dramatic change, as accepted by them and enfolded in their love, our souls found peace and the healing process began.

God's plan, in His own way and His own time, was far better than any we might have devised. Everything we had hoped for on this journey had been denied us: Acceptance; dignity; our sense of professional and personal self-worth. Moreover, the thing we wanted most—a parish ministry. God had made us completely dependent on Him for our life in His church, reminding me that in order to be filled up, we had first to be emptied, letting go to allow Peter's ministry and our lives together, uniquely shared in his priesthood, to be still more deeply touched and transformed. We had said we would go anywhere. Do anything. The rejections, and now the support we received here, with the Benedictine Sisters, were examples of what that meant for us. Normality began trickling back into our lives. The prayers of both communities of sisters supported us through those difficult months and strengthened us in our new ministry.

Peter remained the Benedictine Sisters' permanent Sunday substitute for two years. Without the sensitivity and love of these holy women, he would not have had an altar at which to celebrate Sunday Mass. The Lord had not given us that which we asked, but something much better: grace and peace that enabled us to grow.

Later we became Benedictine Oblates, associates of their community, as they continued to support us with their love and prayers. Our friendship with these women and their example of hospitality and faith gave me the hope I had not dared to long for. And I thought, it is the women—so often the women—who bring reason and wisdom to indifference and suffering.

I recalled the meeting of the Pastoral Provision candidates and their wives in Boston in 1983. There were about twenty couples meeting with the Vatican liaison for the program along with several priests. I remember overhearing one of them comment, "It's the women here who have sacrificed. This is for the women too."

As I thought of his words now with Peter's ordination day behind us, it came to me that perhaps the good of this program will be for the women in the Church. Unlike many Catholic religious women who wanted priesthood for themselves, I simply wanted to be the wife of Peter, a priest, and to fulfill the prayer at our marriage: *"that their home may be a haven of blessing and peace"*. (Marriage Liturgy; Episcopal Book of Common Prayer) Many times Peter had said that he felt his ordination was important for me, that while he was the priest and my life was subordinate to his, in actuality, it was not subordinate at all but central in some way yet unknown to us.

Was what we experienced really rejection or was a married priest and his wife so great an anomaly in the Catholic Church that these things were expected?

I don't know.

I can only say that when priests and religious ignore a bishop's canonical appointments it feels like rejection and it affects not only the priest, but the entire Catholic community.

Did I understand? No, I didn't understand.

It had nothing to do with Jesus and everything to do with human ego. As I had so often, I thought of our children, and the effect our experiences would have on their faith. I hoped that they would look back to the years that formed their faith and find harmony and revelation there. However, I wondered, with all that had happened to their father, would they ever be devout Catholics? Could they know and experience the true richness of faith, as I so wanted for them?

-4-

I had always wanted to write and I thought this might be the time to try so I took a class from Peggy Fielding, at Tulsa Community College. With Peter's encouragement and Peggy's repeated threats that she would write the book if I did not, I began to write the story that had begged to be told for more than five years. When I had fulfilled my one-year commitment to the Sisters of the Sorrowful Mother, I resigned my position to stay home and devote full time to the writing project.

The Sisters asked me to stay and assume greater responsibility in the day-to-day management of the convent. I felt tempted. Still, in one short year, I had become nearly as cloistered and isolated as the retired nuns. Ironically, in trying to free myself of this isolation by working for the Sisters, I unwittingly had slid more deeply into isolation and loneliness. I yearned to create a life with a more normal shape and focus in partnership with Peter's ministry. Like a whirling dervish, I reached out in every direction, searching for that place where I might contribute and feel valued as a woman. With all of this, yet a mystery to me,

I hoped that writing about my experiences and feelings would give me a healthier perspective.

A short time after I left my job at the convent, Brother Lawrence, the director at Bishop Kelley High School called me. "I need an academic secretary in the office. You have a lot of educational experience. Will you come and help us out?" he asked.

"I don't think so. I'm working on a book," I said.

He tried to coax me into working for him, but I held steadfast to my belief that for the moment, I needed to stay at home and write.

A few weeks later, he called again. "I can't find anybody for that job. Are you sure you won't consider helping us?"

"Sorry..." I said.

Within days, he called a third time.

"Could you come part time?"

"Well, I guess I could come and talk to you about it." I had taken one job for the Church without an interview and I did not want to step into another one the same way. However, I felt my resolve to stay at home weakening.

After talking with him, I agreed to work mornings at Bishop Kelley High School. Still, I felt apprehensive about it. I remembered my powerless feelings at the convent. How the job had been what I thought I wanted and how I had found myself with feelings that did not make sense logically. Moreover, I felt fearful of making another mistake. However, I kept these doubts to myself, aware that Peter was not in favor of my working for the Church again.

"You'll never get that book written," Peter admonished when I told him that I thought I would like to take the job.

"I'll feel like I am contributing to our support. I'll be with young people and I've always enjoyed friendships with co-workers." To myself, I argued that I just wanted to be with people. As a Catholic priest's wife and working at home, I was cut off from nearly all social contacts. Also, it was hard to break the emotional dependence of going out to a job every day. I knew it wasn't healthy to spend so much time isolated. But I was afraid to enter yet another Catholic community. Moreover, there was Peter's reluctance. While he did not mention it, I recalled the treatment he had received initially from the Christian Brothers. In my apprehension I worried and fussed. Well, I concluded, there is only one way to find out. I reminded myself that logically, any problems were theirs and not mine, but it always came back to facing my own personal doubts.

I had no reason to fear.

Brother Lawrence Humphrey, whom everyone called Brother Larry, was delighted to have me. That fact alone gave me confidence. The other brothers took their cue from Brother Larry. He was completely up-front with the staff and students, explaining in his informal way how it came to be that a priest could be married. It was the reasonable way to handle my situation and made me feel like a regular person again. Now I would be with students and staff and enjoy interaction with parents. The educational environment was a familiar one for me after working twenty years in the Vashon Island School District. Feeling nourished and more fulfilled than I had anytime since our move to Tulsa five years earlier, I worked in the mornings and returned home each afternoon to work on my book for the remainder of the day.

In these remarkable, literally God-given surroundings, my feelings of isolation began to fade and a sense of normalcy and belonging took their place. Through what seemed almost a miracle—the love and support of the Christian Brothers and the staff—Tulsa finally felt like home.

Brother Larry was a wonderful, funny, robust Friar Tuck sort of person. He was a competent, somewhat disorganized administrator who needed an assistant to keep him sorted out. The education of the students was his first priority, which he artfully mixed with the joy and great fun of life in the Kelley community. I loved it there.

With Brother Larry's love for fun, there was always at least one practical joke floating in the air of the administrative wing of the school. On one occasion, he asked me to complete a report that required the head count of teachers and staff who had been assigned to the school by the Church. On the personnel roster I listed two priests, seven brothers, five nuns, and (with tongue in cheek) one priest's wife. I laid the report on Brother Larry's desk and waited.

"One priest's wife!" he boomed from inside his office.

He laughed wildly, sharing the joke with everyone within earshot. Brother Larry could laugh at the absurd and ridiculous. Left to his own devices, I felt sure he would include me.

When he realized that I was serious about writing a book, he encouraged me and was nearly as excited as I was when Loyola University Press offered me a contract to publish it. I resigned in order to do the rewrites and the publicity, and afterward he asked me to return full time. I accepted. In all, I worked at Bishop Kelley High School for four years.

Shortly after I began thinking about writing a book, and while Peter was a hospital chaplain Paul and Rita Bisdorf walked into our lives. Paul had suffered a stroke and asked for daily Holy Communion. Upon finding out that Peter was married, they asked him to bring me to meet them.

As we left them that day, Peter said to me, "Did you know that Rita wrote for Catholic magazines and newspapers and that Paul has been published?"

"No. I didn't."

"You should talk to Rita about your book. Maybe she would be willing to help you."

"Maybe...." I didn't confess it to even Peter but I wasn't at all sure I wanted a Catholic I didn't know very well involved with my writing. I had little enough confidence as it was.

Each time Peter mentioned the couple or I encountered them at one of his Masses, I thought about her writing background and the possibility of working together. Finally, I got my nerve up and broached the subject with her.

"Can you write?" she asked.

"Well, I don't know. I've started putting down a few things. I could have you look at them, and you can tell me what you think..."

She smiled. "Why don't you mail me a few pages and then we can talk."

"Okay." Still, I felt unsure about this direction. I really wanted objective help but would I be able to take her criticism? Did I know enough about her to trust her? Finally, I didn't want to jeopardize my friendship with her since I had few friends in Tulsa. I stalled and mulled it over in my mind until I had nearly killed the entire project.

Then the phone rang one day and it was Rita. "Mary, did you send me those pages?"

I hesitated. Now I had to admit my cowardice. "No, I haven't. I'm not sure I'm up to this."

"I understand. You know... this is just between us. Nobody besides Paul and Peter needs to know what we're doing. I certainly won't tell. But I don't want to talk you into something you really don't want to do, either."

"Oh, I really want to write it...I think. I'm pretty sure I have a good story to tell." I sent Rita the first pages I'd written. Then I waited.

Several days passed.

I answered the ringing phone to hear Paul's halting speech and excited voice. "Girl, you can write."

Rita got on the line. "Mary, you can do it. I knew you had a story, but I wasn't sure you could tell it. It's wonderful."

From that day Rita and I became closest friends. I wrote and mailed her pieces of the manuscript. When she was ready, we met at her house in Broken Arrow and spent the afternoon at her kitchen table, critiquing and tossing around ideas and impressions about our journey, the Catholic Church, and the priesthood. Paul sat in his recliner well within hearing, his television on mute, and occasionally interjecting his thoughts and conclusions. Rita was an invaluable editor, and I grew to love her as a daughter loves her mother. From these first words placed on the paper to the final acceptance of the galleys and the trauma of seeing my words in print, Rita was my strength and confidante. She never hesitated to support me. Even in the face of criticism and rejections, she never backed away.

-5-

I met with Bishop Beltran to inform him that I was writing a book about our experiences and that I hoped to have it published. "You don't need my approval or anyone else's to write a book about the Church," Bishop Beltran explained.

When the first draft was finished, I gave it to him to read. We discussed it and he made suggestions for revisions. His main concern was that I had used fictitious names for priests and parishes. "If you don't use the true names of people and places, local people will read this book and wonder what else about it isn't true. It is a true story and I believe it should be told. People in Tulsa will recognize who you are talking about anyway and actually, what you're saying isn't that bad."

I felt encouraged when he supported my story and agreed to write the forward.

At about the same time that I contacted Bishop Beltran, I wrote to Cardinal Bernard Law, ecclesiastical liaison to the Vatican for the Pastoral Provision, telling him of my desire to write about our experiences. He did not answer my letter.

Months later when the galleys were ready, I asked Mark, my contact at Loyola University Press, to send a copy to Cardinal Law. I had no idea how Cardinal Law might respond. Still, I loved my Church and I wanted to give the Cardinal the same courtesy that I had extended to Bishop Beltran. More than that, I did not fear Cardinal Law.

Weeks passed and each time I talked to Mark I asked, "Have you heard from Cardinal Law regarding the galley proofs?"

"Not yet," was his consistent answer.

Then in late July, Loyola was ready to print. Mark called me again. "I don't know what to do," he said. "I called Cardinal Law's office and talked to a priest, his public relations secretary, I think. He said that he didn't have time to read the galleys, but when he did, he would determine whether the Cardinal should see them or not."

"Hmmm. Don't call us; we'll call you," I said.

"That's the general idea."

I thought for a moment, frustrated and disappointed in Cardinal Law and the Church. I wanted him to know what I had written. I wanted his blessing but, equally important to me, I wanted to give the Cardinal the opportunity to suggest revisions if he felt that some of the story should not be told. I wanted—needed—to do what I thought was necessary to be a loyal Catholic. I had taken the Church that had once rejected me and I had given it my wholehearted love and support.

Today, I think that they—the hierarchy—had their best opportunity at that moment. If they had only known how much I wanted their participation. I would have done anything they told me to do, including the withdrawal of my book from publication.

Even now, these years later, I don't feel malice toward the hierarchy—only the familiar sadness and disappointment I had known in my childhood. Sadness honed out of a childhood of haves and have-nots, those who possessed the faith and my parents and siblings, who because of my mother's divorce before she married my father, were excluded for reasons not understood by my child mind. I experienced the recurring disappointment that once again I felt pushed aside, a consequence of actions over which I had no control, in this faith I had longed for and, to a degree, had finally won.

I listened to Mark breathing on the other end of the line. I have done everything I know to inform the hierarchy of the book's content, beginning with my letter to Cardinal Law in the first months of the project, I mused.

"Mary? Are you still there?"

"Yes. We've made every effort to do the right thing. Go ahead with it," I said.

As I hung up the phone, I expected that we would hear from Cardinal Law within a day or two. However, weeks passed and no one from his office contacted me.

Then one afternoon in September in my office at Bishop Kelley High School, I received a phone call from Father James Parker, the former Episcopal priest who functioned as Cardinal Law's liaison for the program. Our conversation began with the usual courtesies: "How is Peter? Everything going okay?" A southern gentleman to the core, I thought.

Then he turned to the real purpose of his call. "Cardinal Law read your book, and if you don't mind, he would like me to read it as well."

"Of course." That would be the point, I thought, impatient now with the process.

"Then if I feel as he does about it, we might ask you to change some things."

"Ohhhh."

"Yes. Do you mind?" Father Parker's soft Southern voice was warm and smooth but unmistakably assertive.

"Well, I don't know what to say, Jim."

"What do you mean?"

"The galley proofs have been in Cardinal Law's office for several months. We've tried to get someone there to look at them. Mark, with whom I work at Loyola called his office several times. Then about a month ago he got through to Cardinal Law's secretary who told him that he would determine whether the Cardinal should see them or not."

"Hmmmm. That's unfortunate." He paused. "So at what stage is the process now?"

"I expect the book to be in the stores any day." I hesitated. "You're too late, Jim."

"Oh. Well..."

I was stunned. How could they ignore me for more than a year, and, then on the eve of publication, call me like this?

I drove home in a daze, thinking of Peter's words often repeated during the writing of the book: "They'll never let that book be published."

When I arrived home, I went to the mailbox. There was a package from Loyola. I opened it to find two advance copies of my book. This is a sign, I thought. God does want this book. He has allowed it to happen.

As I held the book in my hands, the reality that my thoughts and words filled its pages was nearly incomprehensible to me. I had done it. I had written it. I had told our story. Here it was.

That day the feeling of accomplishment and pride in my work—regardless of what Cardinal Law and the Church did now—filled me to overflowing with joy. I had carried and given birth to three beautiful children and had raised yet another. Now this book was like a fifth child—finding its source deep within my heart and soul. As with bearing his children, Peter had given me the precious gift of his love and support for this project. Bishop Beltran had encouraged me all the way. I laid the book on the table and smiled as I examined its spine. "Dally" stared boldly back at me. There was the proof. This was my own.

In all that was happening outwardly, there was a lot going on inside me too. Seeing my words in print, especially in a book so personal, was traumatic.

Doubts and questions assailed me in the days prior to the book's appearance in the stores, and I began to feel that if I had known my work would actually be published, I could not have been so open in telling my story. All writing is personal in one way or another. However, a story that is a personal, emotional, and spiritual journey such as ours affected the lives of those I loved most. I was not at all sure that I liked this spotlight and I longed to handle it with grace and poise.

During the days leading up to the launching of the book I tried to prepare myself for my words to become public, when my friends, as well as people I did not know, would read the book. It wasn't just words, but my life and that of my husband and children that would be public knowledge. As a family whose husband and father had been a Protestant minister, now a Catholic priest, our lives had been open to constant scrutiny. Even on Vashon Island, we had had our own fishbowl existence if only a goldfish bowl. There had been times when I had fought fiercely to protect our privacy. While we didn't pretend to be a perfect family, I wanted others to see our good points, not just our faults. Now I realized I had told everything—and to readers who knew nothing about us. I can only say that this book was inside me and it had to come out. If I had ever felt called to anything, I had felt called to write about this period in our lives. This then was authentic to my vocation as a priest's wife. Still, frightened and nervous and, without wanting to, I wondered how my friends and acquaintances in Tulsa would react. Nevertheless, I had to accept that it was done and in God's hands. I had felt called to write it—now it would be up to the Lord to use it for His purpose.

A few days after the book appeared in the stores, I looked up from my work at Bishop Kelley High School to see a priest standing at my desk.

"Will you autograph your book for me, Mary?" he asked.

"How nice of you to come by," I said. Feeling self-conscious, I took the book from his hands.

As I autographed it, the words flowed without effort from my pen and I thought of this young priest who had strengthened and advised us since our arrival in Tulsa six years earlier. I returned the book to him. He read the inscription and smiled. "Thank you, Mary. That's beautiful." Looking up, he asked, "Is there some place we can talk?"

"Why yes..."

I led the way from the administrative office to the main hall. We walked out into the open breezeway connecting the class-rooms and stopped near a concrete bench on the walkway.

He hesitated, then in hardly more than a whisper, he said, "I'm here to ask you not to come to my parish."

His words stung me. Beads of perspiration gathered on my forehead and in the palms of my hands. I felt myself begin to unravel. I wanted to run, to get away from him, to be any other place but here.

I sank down onto the bench. Students around us lingered along the walkways waiting for the final bell to signal their return to class. They seemed not to notice us. The priest's words hung in the air, separating us. Silence penetrated the beautiful afternoon with a sense of foreboding. The seconds dragged. I felt my face grow hot.

"Okay," I said too lightly. I heard my voice, unexpectedly high. Felt my chin tilt a little in defiance. "I just thought...well, I thought it would be enjoyable to attend your parish for one of your Sunday Masses. Then sign books."

I laughed, embarrassed.

I ran my fingers along the edge of the rough stone bench, wanting to move a little away from him. Not wanting my apprehension to get the better of me, I consciously folded my hands in my lap. I watched as the classroom door closed behind the last student at the far end of the breezeway. Time seemed to slow.

"Why?" I asked.

While I waited for his answer, he sat beside me on the garden bench. I felt numb. What did he mean? Not wanted in his parish?

"Why?" I asked a second time.

"The priest I work with doesn't... well, he doesn't like your book," he said finally, almost a whisper.

"Why?" I asked again, turning toward him.

"Well, he doesn't like what you've written about some of the other priests. He does not want you to promote the book in our parish. And—he hesitated—he would prefer not to have it sold there at all."

"I see." I struggled to hold back the lump in my throat, fearing that it would burst forth in a sob. "Has he read the book?" I asked finally.

"No."

"Have you read the book?"

"I've read two of the chapters, and..."

He stopped. I waited for him to continue. A breeze rustled the trees around us in the garden and a few leaves drifted to the ground beneath the statue of St. John Baptist De La Salle. The breeze caught my hair and gently cooled my face.

"Well, I have to say that I thought it was offensive. However, if it were up to me I would not keep you out of the parish." He looked away. "I—I have to honor my brother priest's request."

"I see."

I had respected this young priest. I could hardly believe what I heard. That he had censored a book, any book. But, a book he had not read?

"Why did you name names?" he asked, ending the awkward silence.

I had not expected this from this priest.

Why am I always "not expecting" these things? I asked myself. Of course, I should have expected it: it's what the book is about. Fitting in. Half-truths. The boys' club.

My body relaxed a bit and I felt the sun on my skin again. I reminded myself that Oklahoma had become my home and it was good to be here, to feel the sun and the cooling breeze.

Ours was a true story. I had not thought everyone would like it, but I had hoped other Catholics would respect its integrity and possibly come to respect me for having the courage to tell it.

"Why did you use names?" the priest asked me a second time.

I wonder now why I bothered to explain, but I began: "When I wrote the first draft, I used fictitious names for the parishes, priests, and sisters in Tulsa. However—" I turned to him and smiled, "—I would be the first to say that there was no way to disguise them—to people who know them—and still tell the story. They are all too well known. When I asked Bishop Beltran to read the first draft of the manuscript, he suggested that I use actual names because he felt that readers would identify the people anyway and the strength of the story is that it is true. There is the feeling..." I hesitated, looked into his face, wanting him to understand. "There is a feeling that if you insert something that is obviously not true, the reader asks: What else about this book isn't true? I simply wanted to tell the truth of what happened and how it affected me. I know that some things about certain people are not flattering, but then, the images of Peter and me are not always flattering either. It's the truth of my personal experience. Some truths are beautiful. Some are not."

"Hmmm."

Again, the silence.

"I must admit I had mixed feelings about using the names." I looked up when I heard the gym door open. A group of students burst out onto the sidewalk, laughing and talking. I watched them—a living organism—the future Catholic Church.

"I thought and prayed about it for a long time. In the end, it seemed that the Bishop's advice was the right way to go. That using the names supported the integrity I hoped to achieve. I did not want to damage anyone's reputation or ministry. There are things I could have said that would have done that. I just wanted to tell the story as honestly as I could. I tried to tell it with love."

I twisted the wooden beads around my neck. Peter had bought them for me at Lazarus' tomb when we had made our pilgrimage to the Holy Land. "Only one American dollar!" I could still hear the street peddler's voice. A trinket, yet it symbolized many things in my life. Peter, my husband. His priesthood. Healing. And life out of death. What more could I say to this priest than what I had already said?

I was suddenly overcome with the feeling that I had failed in writing the book. That it's not all right to be humanly flawed. That truth has no honor.

Conflicting images assaulted me.

I felt the silence close in around me. Fidgeted. Looked down at my hands and turned them. I bit my lower lip. I would not let him see me cry. Finally able to smile, I turned to face him. In a whisper I asked, "Has someone said that what I've written isn't true?"

This was what I really feared.

"No. No one has said that."

Knots tightened in my stomach. A bitter taste filled my mouth. I tried to concentrate on breathing. No words would come. Why didn't he leave? The second group of students had returned to class now. The walkway was quiet. I visualized drinking gulps of water. Not to cry. Not to lose my dignity. Remember who I am. What I represent.

"Have you talked to Bishop Beltran?" I asked.

"Yes, I went to see him."

"Did he tell you he had read all the drafts?"

"He said it didn't look as bad on the typed page as it did in print."

I smiled at the absurdity of his words. "Then you know all of this."

"I'm sorry, Mary. We do not want you to publicize the book, nor do we want it sold in the parish."

"All right." Then, as though from a distance, I heard myself say, "I won't come."

"This priest you've written about..." He gestured with the book. "Do you think you could talk to him—explain how it happened that you used names? Could you apologize? Perhaps that would make things a bit better." He waited for my answer. "Do you think you could do that, Mary?" Something in his patronizing manner and his voice seemed to mock me. I wanted to get away from him more than ever.

Then I heard myself say, "I don't mind talking to him. But, what would I say? That I'm sorry? I'm not sorry. Would I say I lied? I didn't lie. I simply wrote the facts as I experienced them." Tears threatened to surface. I fought to hold them back. I blinked and dabbed at my face with the back of my hand. Wiped it on my skirt.

"I can't believe how naïve I am. I had actually hoped that writing this story—telling it with charity and love—would be healing for all of us." I laughed at my naiveté about the Tulsa priest, the man who had tried to prevent Peter's ordination, who had said we were not fit for this task.

"But the priests aren't against Peter because he is married." The priest smiled. I thought, if marriage has nothing to do with it, why bring it up at all?

I faced him, my pain now turned to anger, and I felt a flood of relief as I allowed myself the luxury to feel it. "No. I won't come to your parish. Thanks for coming to me personally, though. You should read the book. Since you haven't, well, I don't know what to think."

I stood to say good-bye to this priest whom I had regarded as a friend. I looked into his face. I saw deep sadness there. We both knew things had changed. I hesitated. Was there something more I should say? Then I reminded myself of what he had done, and he hadn't even read the book.

I walked slowly past the classrooms and felt his eyes follow me. Students and teachers' voices drifted through the open windows along the breezeway. I had no tears now. But, I wondered, how would I tell Lois, the owner of Catholic Book and Gift, that I wouldn't be going with her Sunday.

And then I knew.

I had to tell her the truth.

(Author's note: In the following years, this priest repeatedly asked me if I had apologized to the priest I had written about. Each time I told him that I had not. As time passed and I understood our place in the Catholic Church more clearly, I wondered about the other priest's lack of hospitality and charity toward us, his effort to deny Peter his priestly vocation. I wondered: If an apology were due, were we not entitled to one?)

"For I was hungry and you gave me no food,
I was thirsty and you gave me no drink,
a stranger and you gave me no welcome..."

Matthew 25:43

-6-

This was not to be the end of the priests' challenges for me. A few days later, I learned that a group of them were putting pressure on Ziegler's Catholic Supply store in Tulsa by threatening to take their business, worth hundreds of thousands of dollars each year, to an out-of-town Catholic supplier if Ziegler's sold my book from their store.

This was the last thing I had expected.

What was there about me—about my book—that brought fire to the bellies of these priests? I had not intended to be a source of rancor and contention in the church.

These priests were the readers I had thought would be most open—my husband's brothers in Christ—those men who could most relate to our experiences of delay and rejection, of political intrigue and of personal grudges.

How wrong I had been.

Naively I had hoped that telling our story would open the door to their understanding of the journey we had made and the reasons we had embarked upon it.

How often I had waited with others outside the confessional, in awe of this uniquely Catholic expression of our common sinfulness. How often I had marveled that through this awkward experience, so many received God's healing grace in the sacrament of forgiveness.

Now, this image mocked my faithfulness.

Angry and hurt, I telephoned my son John in Seattle. He worked for Viking Penguin, a New York publishing house, and I hoped he could advise me. "They're taking my book and twisting it into something evil, John. They don't even read it. They gossip among themselves and then they dissect it by reading only what they consider to be the juicy parts."

I could hear a concerned smile in his voice as he said, "People have been reading only the juicy parts of books since the invention of the printing press. A book belongs to the author until it is in print and then it belongs to whoever picks it up to read. You have to let it go now, Mom."

"But they admit they haven't even read it."

"It's out of your control, Mom. There is nothing you can do. You didn't mean to cause mayhem, but maybe in the long run it will be good. And don't worry about Dad." John laughed. "You've made the best of situations he's created. It's your turn now. He can take care of himself."

"How could I have been so stupid?" I asked. Still, despite my discomfort I knew that he was right. I needed to let go. I had to let the book be what it was regardless of the outcome. "I suppose you're right."

Only the silence of the long distance telephone line lay between us as I let the reality of his words seep into my being, restoring balance to my battered emotions.

"You did a great job, Mom. You should be proud of your work."

I heard my son's voice calling me back to this moment of achievement and celebration. I would have to let it be, take each day as it came, knowing that only God's love is perfection.

"I'm really proud of you, Mom. A lot of people think they can write a book, but they don't do it. And this is a good book."

A few days later Peter said he needed to go to Ziegler's to buy candles. "Mary, don't you think you should go with me to see if those priests has really threatened Ziegler's?" Peter asked. I heard tenderness in his voice.

"I have no idea what will happen there. I suppose anything is possible."

"You might as well get it over with and find out for sure."

"Well, I do need to know how far this has gone. For one thing, it's embarrassing. The store ordered a large number of copies and if they decide not to sell them, Loyola does not allow returns. I guess for my own sense of right I need to know if the priests have carried out their threat."

"If they feel they can't sell them, maybe you could buy them yourself so they don't suffer the loss."

"I guess..." I sighed. What next?

I was only slightly relieved when the book department manager greeted us with a smile. "One of the priests was in yesterday and said that he has read your book, and it is okay for us to sell it." She named the priest who had come to see me at Bishop Kelley High School. "We've put it back out in the store," she said with a satisfied smile. Clearly, she expected her words to please me.

I looked in the direction she pointed. I did not see the table display that we had discussed, but one copy discreetly placed among other titles on a low shelf.

So, it was true; they had threatened to boycott, I thought. I wanted to fight back, to point out that Bishop Beltran had written the foreword. I wanted to ask why it took that priest's approval for this store to sell my book. I wanted to ask why she had practically hidden my book from public view. But I didn't. I did not want to create more tension with Ziegler's or the priests than already existed. Somehow, I doubted that these priests were finished with me. They were angry and I was sure that I had not heard the last of them. I turned to her. "Thank you," I said.

Of course, the boycott rumors created far more interest than might normally have occurred. The word spread that Catholic Book and Gift and Steve's Sundries had a good supply, and my readership grew in spite of, or perhaps because of, the priests' efforts.

I received a phone call one day from a young Tulsa woman. "I wonder if you have thought of withdrawing your book from publication?" she asked.

"No," I said. "Why would I do that?"

"Well, it's against the Church to say or print anything negative about our priests. And anyway it isn't true what you said about that priest who didn't want Father Peter to be ordained."

They don't get it, I thought. The Bishop saw the book before it was submitted to a publisher. He knew the story better than anyone and he chose to write the forward. Still this person was telling me it's against the Church.

"Have you read the book?" I asked.

"Well, I read the lies you wrote about him."

"And how do you know they're lies?"

"He says it isn't true," was her quick response.

"But, how do *you* know it isn't true?" I repeated.

"He says he didn't know you were coming to his parish."

"I have our letters to him and the responses we received from Bishop Beltran and the vicar general. We talked with his staff and we had Father Peter's books shipped there with his permission."

When she didn't reply, I asked, "Do you really think I would write something I can't back up with written documentation?"

"Oh..."

I continued. "In any case, the publication rights don't belong to me. They belong to Loyola University Press. It's not within my power to withdraw the book. I wouldn't, even if I could."

"Some of the priests are going to sue you," she said.

"I guess they can try."

Of course, I thought. What next?

In the midst of all this, another figure appeared without notice in my office at Bishop Kelley High School. "I've come to have you autograph your book for me." When I looked up I saw that the voice belonged to a priest.

"I'd be happy to," I said, but I wondered what this was really all about and I feared more retribution from another member of the brotherhood. My hand shook as I wrote the inscription to him. "Thank you, Father." I handed the book back.

"It's going to be a Catholic classic, you know." He smiled. "It's a good book."

And then he turned and walked out of the building. My body went limp as I watched him go. Tears stung my eyes, and this time I did not try to hold them back.

I knew it took courage for him to come, still more to make this gesture of support.

Months later, a priest friend invited us to his rectory for dinner. He asked me about book sales.

I said, "Very well, but I still don't understand why it caused a big fuss. I naively thought it would be taken in the spirit of truth and love—a difficult journey, but one that had personal meaning for us and the Diocese of Tulsa, as well as the whole Church."

"You broke the code of silence," he said with a smile.

"The code of silence?" I asked.

"It's the idea that what goes on inside the priesthood stays there—not to be publicized or talked about," he said. "It's a sickness in our Church. It needs to change."

How right he is, I thought.

Even in all this, I found myself touched by the amazing goodness of people as I accepted invitations to receptions and other events. I went through book signings and interviews with an outer poise and confidence that I did not feel inside. I appeared on television in Boston and Seattle and accepted opportunities for radio interviews, including National Public Radio. The book was reviewed in nearly every Catholic publication I had ever heard of and some I hadn't. One such publication was *Our Sunday Visitor*, said to be the nation's most widely circulated Catholic weekly.

After years of sitting on the distaff side of Peter's ministry, I found it a bit overwhelming. I had thought there would be brief attention to the book. However, dreamlike, it continued. I did not recover from my wonder that something I had written was actually published and that it had garnered so much attention. More incredible were the warm letters I received from devout Catholics all over the country. There were hundreds of them.

I was again honored when in 1989 the Oklahoma Writers Federation selected me for the "Okie Award", naming the book the Best Non-fiction Book by an Oklahoma Writer that year.

I wondered how I could live up to these honors and attention. I had planned to follow this book with a memoir of our years after Peter's ordination. However, as the priests continued their efforts against me, I could not help but wonder how this would affect my ability to write openly in the future. And what about Peter's ministry? Would this affect his relationship with the other priests? While some denied it, others said it was obvious that my book created some problems for Peter.

As the weeks became months, I thought interest in my book would lessen. However, requests continued to come from laypersons in both the Episcopal and Catholic Churches.

One day at my office at Bishop Kelley High School, I received a call from a young Catholic woman who attended a Tulsa parish. She invited me to speak at their women's club several months later, and I accepted.

Shortly before the date arrived, she called me again. She said, "I'm really sorry, but we got mixed up and somehow we have two speakers scheduled for that meeting."

I thought she would suggest an alternate date. When she did not, I said, "It's your priest, isn't it? I thought he might do this."

"I'm very sorry," she said.

"It's not your fault," I assured her.

When I hung up the phone, the secretary who sat at the desk next to mine said, "Don't tell me..."

"The women's club didn't run it by their priest before they invited me to speak."

Perhaps my most cherished moment came when I received a scribbled note from a priest who had had his larynx removed because of throat cancer. It said, "Give 'em hell, sweetheart."

-7-

Holy Family Cathedral

Tulsa, Oklahoma

1987

"Guess what I heard today?" Peter closed the front door and gave me a hurried kiss on the cheek. Laying his black corduroy coat over a chair, he sat down at our dining room table.

"Father West congratulated me—says I'm going to be the associate pastor at Holy Family Cathedral."

"Oh?"

He reached for the bowl of crackers and crumbled a handful into his soup. "Says he heard it from another priest."

Although the cathedral pastor had frequently called Peter to fill in as a Mass celebrant, we did not expect a permanent assignment there.

"Do you think there's anything to it?" I asked.

"I don't know."

Three weeks passed and we heard nothing more.

Then Peter received a call from Bishop Beltran's secretary asking him to come to the bishop's office the following day.

Bishop Beltran greeted Peter with a warm smile. "I have thought from the time I first met you and Mary that you belong in a parish ministry. I want you to go to Holy Family Cathedral as the associate pastor."

"You do remember what happened the last time you assigned me there, don't you?"

"Now, Peter, you must be forgiving."

"I'd like very much to be in parish ministry, but Father Gray turned me away two years ago. I can't imagine him wanting me there now." Peter laughed. "Anyway, the Pastoral Provision does not permit married priests to serve in full time parish ministries."

"I want you to go there. Father Gray has agreed to it. Besides, your individual decretal does not say that you may not be in a parish so we're going to put you there and see what happens. Your title will be associate pastor. The people would not understand anything else."

"Well, okay..."

"I know you will like it there and you will like working with this particular priest."

When Peter came home, he told me what Bishop Beltran had said.

"It's true then—we are to be in a parish." I was delighted.

"We'll see. You know how it was the last time Bishop assigned me there."

We were seated at our dining room table in the house on 17th Place and Wheeling where we had lived since 1983. Earlier in the spring, I had planted marigolds and they were in full bloom, a mass of orange and gold, dramatic against the weathered wood fence. Peter looked out into the yard. "Gosh, those marigolds are beautiful. At least we won't have to move. So if it doesn't work out that won't be a problem."

"I wouldn't mind moving."

"No need to even think about it. The cathedral is only a couple of miles away." Peter had a way of bringing me back to the present moment and dismissing any thoughts I might have about a move.

"I like this house but...."

An older house built in the 1930s, the kitchen and bathroom had been remodeled and updated. The Sisters had offered it to us to rent with pleasure because it was one of the nicest houses they owned. However, the house did not feel right to me. Worse, I could not say why. Something about the house had made me uneasy, beginning with the first day there. I felt sure it had been a place of pain and tragedy. Peter, like most men, paid little attention to my uneasiness.

When we had been there several years I met a former occupant who asked me, "Is the ghost still in that house?"

"Ghost? I haven't seen it but I know there's something," I said, grateful that someone else had felt the presence.

"I used to actually see the ghost in the bathroom. We were told that someone died under uncertain circumstances there," she explained, confirming what I already felt.

"I meet with the pastor on Friday." Peter brought me back to the present, having already put to rest my desire to move to another house. "I'm not holding my breath."

Later, after the meeting, Peter told me that he was hardly aware of the 103-degree temperature as he walked across the parking lot toward the cathedral. He stood at the locked iron gate that guarded the entry to the cathedral offices and wondered what the next hour would bring. He could not help feeling apprehensive. He took a deep breath and rang the bell.

"Yes?" A woman's voice came over the intercom.

"It's Father Dally. I have an appointment with Father Gray."

The gate buzzed to release the lock, and Peter stepped inside. He walked through the small cloistered garden, and as he approached the locked door to enter the office area, the lock clicked and he turned the knob. The secretary emerged around the corner to direct him to the pastor's office in the large turn-of-the-century downtown church.

"Father is waiting for you," she said.

A moment later, the good-looking white-haired priest rose from his desk and extended his hand. "Glad to see you."

"Thank you, Father."

"George. Call me George."

"Thank you."

"Sit down. Sit down." In the small office, Father Gray motioned toward the couch against the wall opposite his desk.

Peter looked around the room. Bookcases covered one wall of the tidy professional workspace. His habit of scanning the backs of books momentarily interrupted his train of thought as he identified familiar theological titles. "Nice library."

"My books are about the only things here that reflect my taste. My sister had her decorator come in a few years ago. I'm not much good at those things myself."

"It's very nice."

Father smiled. "Well, a woman's touch makes it feel homey."

"Yes. I had forgotten that you have family here."

"I don't see them very often but we usually get together on holidays. It's nice to be near them."

Peter nodded. "Mary misses our family."

"Yes. Well. Let's talk about your work here." He looked up from his desk. "Now, you will have the associate's office just down the hall. We'll take a look at it in a few minutes. It needs painting; we didn't do anything to it when we redecorated. I can't remember why. I'll have it painted before you start. Then, I want you to go to—I can't think of the name of that furniture store—it's down on Harvard Avenue at about 41st Street, I think. You'll find it. I want you to go and get yourself a desk. Pick out anything you like and charge it to the cathedral account."

"Thank you. I'll take Mary with me."

"Now about your day off. Most of the priests take Monday. However, I want someone here on Mondays to take calls and such, so you may take any other day. Uh, except Saturday or Sunday, of course." We later learned that it is rare for the Tulsa priests not to share the same day off each week.

"Mary has Thursday off at Bishop Kelley High School so I'd like to take Thursday, if that's all right."

"Fine. Fine. Now, I want you to start right away, I can't re-member the exact date the Bishop said, but you received a letter too didn't you? Look at the letter. It has the date. I don't have anybody right now to help me. I'll have the women put on a reception for you and your wife. We don't usually do that for a new associate, but I think since you have, uh, unusual circumstances, it will be a good thing to do. Now, let's take a look at that office and I want you to meet the staff."

Peter said that the associate's office appeared not to have been in use for some time. The air smelled stale and the paint and draperies were faded and dusty. There was a small desk and chair. Peter started to sit in the chair, thinking it might be suitable for the new desk. "Don't sit down—you'll get your suit filthy. The last associate didn't use this office at all," Father explained. "I want you to meet the staff."

Peter followed Father Gray down the hall. "This is Dorothy, the parish secretary and in here is Mary, our accountant. I think you've met Sister Eugenia, our director of religious education. This is her office. Then, of course, we have Father Co and Father Kirley who are both retired. Both priests help out with the Mass schedule, but they don't do any other work in the parish."

"Let's go to the kitchen. John is our maintenance man and Olivia is the rectory cook. You'll get to know them too."

Peter liked Olivia, an African American, instantly.

He later met Farrell Dixon, organist and choir director, and Donna Reneau, cantor; both were Episcopalians who later converted to Catholicism.

As Father Gray had planned, the Women's Club held a reception to welcome us. In his homily, he introduced us and told the people at each Mass a little about Peter's background. Father

Gray explained the Pastoral Provision and how, under these special conditions, a priest could be married and have a family. Like Brother Larry, he honored our marriage and Peter's priesthood by being totally open and direct.

I wondered why Father Gray and Brother Larry realized this and others did not. How many misunderstandings and awkward situations for us, as well as for others, had resulted from fear that lay persons would not understand this exception to the rule of celibacy?

Since first entering the program, we had been repeatedly cautioned and counseled by priests and sisters that the laity would not welcome a married priest; that we should prepare for criticism and possible disapproval. With this warning, it was with cautious optimism that I began my days as the wife of the associate pastor at Holy Family Cathedral.

However, not only did we experience warmth and gestures of friendship and support from laypersons in general, but conservative Catholics welcomed us as well. We had been told that a married priest would certainly upset them. Throughout out ministry we experienced the warmth and support of lay Catholics everywhere.

-8-

For the first time since we became Catholics, I did not feel self-conscious about my presence in the Church. Because of Father Gray's openness, I no longer needed to explain myself, nor did I fear that I might be an embarrassment to the Church. It was a blessing and a relief to enter a new life through this uncomplicated acceptance and the dignity Father Gray allowed me to enjoy as a woman and priest's wife. It was not that he approved. I felt sure he did not. He never called me by name and I often felt like a woman without a face. However, he accepted us and made the best of what he must have considered an awkward situation. We were welcomed and valued from our first Sunday there and we loved the people and staff in return.

After several months, it was easy to set aside the events of two years earlier when Bishop Beltran had assigned Peter to the cathedral the first time and Father Gray had turned him away.

We had been at the cathedral short time when Father Gray invited us to the rectory for dinner. When we arrived, the three priests and another visiting priest were seated and had started dinner without us.

Peter explained, "The telephone rang just as we were leaving the house. It was our daughter, Monica, calling from the Caribbean. I'm sorry we're late. We got here as soon as we could."

"Dinner begins at six o'clock," Father Grey said. He appeared irritated, or perhaps I interpreted this in my anxiety with the situation. Olivia appeared in the doorway with full plates of pork roast, green beans, mashed potatoes, and gravy. Her eyes got big and her mouth flew open at Father Gray's words. She placed the heaping plates on the table and turned to go, but not before she turned to us and rolled her eyes.

I said, "I'm really sorry." I looked around the table at each of the four priests, realizing that they could not understand how it might be to have your schedule interrupted by a son or daughter. "It's so hard to make contact with her at the hospital where she is a volunteer that we couldn't very well..." My voice trailed off to uneasy silence as I realized they had closed their minds to anything I might say.

Olivia came back into the room carrying our salads. "Things happen like that when you got children. Isn't that right, Father Gray?" I felt the reassuring touch of her hand on my shoulder as she placed the salad next to my plate.

He smiled. "Well...I wouldn't know."

I told myself that I was reading too much into his words when the visiting priest said, "I hear you're writing a book, Mary." *(Author's Note: this event occurred prior to the book's publication date.)*

"Yes..."

"What is it about?"

I fumbled with my silverware and glanced toward Peter sitting next to me but he appeared not to notice. "I guess you would say it's autobiographical." I smiled.

"Oh, really?"

"It's the story of our journey from the Episcopal to the Catholic Church. It ends with Peter's ordination."

"I see... Have you training to write this book?" His smile seemed to mock me.

"I like to write and...." I laughed nervously. "...I know the story better than anyone else."

"I see."

This priest was respected and revered by both clergy and lay people. Still, there was no kindness in his tone—nor was there warmth in his eyes.

I concentrated on my food and tried to bolster my self-confidence. Could I have misunderstood the tone of his questions? Perhaps they were upset only because we were late. It seemed rude to me that they had begun to eat before we arrived. I had expected a rectory to operate like any household. Later, I realized that most rectories are institutional in this respect. Dinner begins at six o'clock whether everyone is there or not. I was wrong to be offended because they had not waited for us. It had nothing to do with Peter and me joining them for dinner.

Meanwhile Peter, beside me, appeared to take little notice of the conversation. Later I would learn that he had become accustomed to this priest's battering ram of challenges and put-downs, so much so that he often ate in the kitchen to avoid the unpleasantness. This night was an education for me as more than two years after Peter's ordination, this was my first exposure to dinner with priests in a rectory setting.

Father Kirley turned to Father Gray and said, "I think it's a remarkable thing Peter and Mary have done. Don't you, George?"

The room was silent.

Father Gray picked up his dinner napkin and touched his lips, then laid it on the table. "Yes. It takes courage." He turned to me. "That's what it is: courageous." He smiled.

After dinner, Peter and I strolled across the parking lot toward our car. I felt the discomfort of the August heat and humidity that hung in the air even though the sun had set. Temperatures of 105 degrees or more radiated from the asphalt pavement, typical for Tulsa in late summer.

Leaving the cathedral, we turned left onto 10th Street and passed the building that had once been a Jewish synagogue. The congregation had outgrown the facility years earlier and built a new synagogue and community center near Utica Square, the city's prestigious residential and shopping district.

I thought of the story Peter loved to tell about the man from Chicago who came to Tulsa in the 1920's to interview for the position of rabbi at one of the temples. The search committee interviewed several qualified candidates but they really liked the rabbi from Chicago. When they asked him if he was married, he told them that he was not.

"But, Rabbi, how can you know the joys and the sorrows of our lives if you have no wife and children of your own? We are very sorry, but we want our rabbi to be a family man."

The rabbi said, "Can you wait just one week to make your decision?"

The committee agreed to wait. The rabbi returned to Chicago and went to see his long-time girlfriend. He said to her, "Ruth, it's time we got married."

Lucky for the rabbi, Ruth agreed, and the next week they traveled to Tulsa.

"Gentlemen, I'd like you to meet my soon-to-be wife."

The committee members nodded and smiled in Hebraic agreement. "Welcome. We want you to be our Rabbi," they said.

The rabbi and his wife served the Jewish synagogue for thirty years. They became loved and revered members of the Tulsa community.

Perhaps this story was apocryphal. It did not matter. I smiled to myself and thought of this practical Jewish approach to a celibate or married clergy.

I turned to Peter. "You know, Catholics have a lot to learn."

"Hmmm."

"Father Gray is such a gracious man. However, let's face it. He's clueless when it comes to marriage and women."

"Clueless?"

"I felt bombarded by the negative energy at dinner tonight."

"They're trying to make us feel welcome."

"I wonder."

"Mary, those men are very much in tune with the politics of the Catholic Church. You really can't blame them."

"I remember what Bishop Beltran said to us."

"About what?"

"Remember? He said it several times: You have no idea how unusual this is."

"Unusual? Yes." Peter turned the car into our driveway. "It's probably pretty unusual to invite a woman to the rectory for a meal too, don't you think?"

"I never thought of that," I said. "I'll bet you're right."

-9-

Father Kirley was an Irishman who loved his whiskey and his piano. He played superbly regardless of his condition. He regarded Father Gray's vacations as his opportunity to have a party. St. Patrick's Day was approaching and, being a proper Irishman, he suggested to me that I might cook and serve a luncheon for a few of his friends after the noon Mass on that festive day.

Father Kirley confided, "I can't ask Olivia to take on additional duties. I might have four or five priests come. And Peter, of course."

"Okay, Father. I'll do it. I love parties."

A few days later, he stopped me in the hall at the rectory. "Can you get some decorations? We can't really celebrate without a few table favors."

"Yes, I'll go down to Ehrle's Party Store and see what they have," I said.

"I knew you'd understand. You don't mind, do you?" It was not a question, but a declaration of the attitude I should assume regarding his party. And, of course, I truly did not mind.

Actually, I was flattered and looked upon it as an opportunity to become friends with the priests at the cathedral as well as those who attended.

Several days before the luncheon, Father Kirley called me. "We might have one or two more for lunch."

"Fine," I said. To myself I thought, that means possibly eight for lunch.

Peter came home from the church the next evening and said, "Mary, you'd better get a definite number from Father Kirley for that luncheon. It sounds to me like things are getting out of hand. You know how he is. I think he has delusions of grandeur. With Father Gray gone he seems to be taking over the operation of the cathedral."

"Did Father Gray leave him in charge?"

"Good Lord, no. But he's into the sauce and he thinks he's running the place..."

"After the last time he increased the number I was afraid this might happen. What should I do?"

"You better call him," Peter said. "Be firm with him now."

"That's easy for you to say." I grimaced at the thought of what it might take to be firm with this charming old Irishman.

When I called Father Kirley, he said, "Well, there might be a few more. But that won't bother you, will it?"

"I just want to be sure we have enough food, Father. I don't want you to be embarrassed if we're short. Besides, it would ruin my reputation." I laughed.

"You can charge everything you need at Petty's."

"I know, but I need to know how many I'm going to serve."

"Well, let's say...twenty?"

I had already made a second trip to Ehrle's for more decorations. To be safe, I'd go one more time. I decided too, that I needed to have a little chat with Olivia, the cook.

"Father Kirley's party for three or four friends has turned into lunch for twenty. What shall I do?" I asked her as we sat at her kitchen table in the rectory.

"Mmmm-mm. Honey, you got to know that Father Kirley don't wait for the dust to settle after Father Gray backs out of his garage before he gets a party together. This time he's been leanin' on his old friend, Mr. Johnnie Walker!"

"I hate not knowing how many will show up. He says twenty but I don't feel comfortable because he keeps adding priests. I could end up with more like thirty guests. Lucky for me corned beef and cabbage is easy."

"Honey, you got to learn sometime!" Olivia whooped and laughed, wiping the tears from her eyes and holding her ample sides.

"If I make a mess of this, those priests will be gloating for years to come. There are a few who would love to see me fall flat on my face."

"...member, now, if you too good, they's goin' to want more parties by Mary." Olivia whooped and laughed again, rolling her eyes and shaking her head.

"No way. Once is enough."

"Honey, those priests tries to make every woman their slave. Truth is, most women likes it. They jus' loves to do for a priest."

"Well, I'll prepare food for thirty just to be sure. Keep your ear to the ground now, Olivia. If you hear or see anything I should know, please call me. See you later. And thanks for the great lunch."

"Like I says, while the cat's away them mice do play! Mmmmmmm." I heard Olivia laugh as I left through the back door. I smiled, thinking what a great friend she was to Peter and me.

St. Patrick's Day arrived and the noon Mass at Holy Family was packed. I had decorated the Green Room in the church basement and the meal was prepared, but I was nervous. I had set aside extra cabbage and Irish soda bread, noting on the table across the room that Father Kirley had plenty of drinks on hand. At the last minute I added all the extra cabbage to the corned beef, stretching food for thirty to serve a final thirty-four hungry priests.

The party seemed to be a success. When Father Kirley thanked me with a gift of a leather bound book of Irish poetry, I was sure I had made a friend.

When Father Gray came home the next week, I feared I'd be in trouble over the extra food I had charged at Petty's Grocery, but he didn't say a word.

A few weeks later, I invited Father Kirley to come to our home for dinner.

"Oh, I couldn't do that," he said. He seemed anxious as he looked around to see if anyone was near by.

"Peter can come and get you and take you home after dinner, if you don't drive."

"No, that's not it," he said. "If I go to your house, the other priests will get after me. You see, they won't like it. I just can't do it."

Fine, I thought. I can run all over Tulsa and do your parties, but Peter and I are outcasts. I was furious. They didn't like a priest being married, but I could be his secret girlfriend and they would look the other way. It was all backwards from the way it was supposed to be. And I felt as I had so many times, that it was important not to be too good at anything. They would tolerate us as long as, in their eyes, we didn't succeed.

I recalled my Black friend Merylin saying to me one day, "Mary, I'm a prophet, you know."

"Oh really?" I asked, smiling.

"Yeah. I think Father Peter is going to be the next pastor of Holy Family Cathedral."

"Oh no, Merylin. We wouldn't want that."

"Why?" she asked, baffled.

"Well, because, you know that in order to be as good as they are, we have to be better. Please don't wish that on us."

"Oh, I know. You got what I got."

"What's that?"

"Prejudice."

We both laughed, but it was true. I had begun to realize that there was no way we would ever be accepted by these priests. We were just too different.

As my anger toward Father Kirley and my feelings of humiliation melted away, I forgave him. What was there not to forgive? He seemed unaware that he had done or said anything to offend me. I didn't expect an apology anyway. I had learned through other experiences that priests rarely say they're sorry.

I wanted to at least be congenial with priests who were my husband's brothers in Christ, but there seemed no way to establish normal friendships with them. They didn't know who we were in their system. Here it was again—that business of fitting in. Clearly, we did not.

I wondered what the priests had expected to happen when the bishop polled them and they agreed to welcome a priest and his wife. Did they not expect us to be a part of the life of the diocese? Few of them seemed to have the desire to reach beyond their own experiences. Few seemed to have the ability, or more possibly, the desire to think creatively enough to include us in an appropriate way. We were all victims of this antiquated Roman system. Peter and I needed to fit in. Nevertheless, I was learning that, in fact, we would never be a normal part of the clerical life in the Catholic Church.

During the remainder of our life and ministry in Oklahoma, when Peter suggested we invite a priest to our home for dinner, Father Kirley's words, returned to fill me with sadness and doubt: "If I go to your house the other priests will get after me. They won't like it.".

-10-

"Does Father really want to room with his mother?" the pilgrimage director asked.

"Oh, you must mean Mary Dally," Dorothy, Father Gray's secretary responded.

"Yes..."

"Well, actually she's his wife." Both, Dorothy, the secretary and Mary, the accountant, enjoyed the anomaly of having a married priest on the staff. Dorothy laughed as she explained to the travel agent our unusual situation.

The cathedral choir had invited Peter to accompany them on their singing tour of Italy. I was excited and when I registered for the trip, I indicated that I would like to room with Father Peter. It seemed that I was constantly required to explain our situation and sometimes, I simply rebelled inwardly, thinking 'let them ask'.

In Rome, the group connected with the Italian tour director. As the trip continued, he turned up everywhere. Across cathedral naves, on street corners, at every street kiosk, across restaurants and museums, there he was. At each event, I would look up only to see him look away. At first I tried to speak to him. Concerned about scandal, I wanted to reassure him of our particular situation. However, he avoided me at every turn. I concluded that it was his problem, and I resolved to have a good time and not to worry.

The choir had been invited to sing the Mass in St. Peter's Basilica on the first Monday in Advent. When we arrived, we were met by Father Tam, a priest from the Diocese of Tulsa who was in residence at the Gregorian College working on an advanced theological degree. "Come on, Peter, I'll take you back to the sacristy where the priests are vesting." He motioned for Peter to follow him.

"I don't know what I'm doing. I'd be happy just to stay with Mary." Peter turned to me. "Will you be safe here?" There was an almost comic plea in his manner.

I laughed and said, "Oh, for heaven's sake, go."

St. Peter's, the seat of Roman Catholicism, is the most visited Christian religious site in the world. I could only think of the tremendous honor and excitement I hoped Peter would feel assisting at this Mass in this church that most symbolized the Holy Father and Roman Catholicism. However, I knew that elaborate liturgical ceremonies made him nervous and I understood his hesitancy.

In the sacristy, Peter and our Tulsa friend encountered a large group of priests and bishops. He told me later that it wasn't clear to him who was in charge. Still more confusing for Peter, they all spoke Italian, including Father Tam, a Vietnamese priest. After a time, a priest pointed to Peter. "Me?" he asked. He felt a gentle push from Father Tam who nodded and motioned for Peter to join the procession.

He turned to Father Tam. "I'd rather stay in the congregation...."

"Don't worry, Peter. Just go over there and stand with that priest. All you have to do is follow him."

As the Mass began, I could not see Peter anywhere. Then I spotted him near the back of the procession. With an uncertainty that was obvious only to me, Peter moved into his assigned role. I prayed for him and hoped that when it was over, he would reflect with satisfaction on the exceptional honor it signified for a priest who is also a husband and father.

It was then that I began to wonder what the occasion for this Mass might be. We knew only that the cathedral choir would sing the Mass. However, it had to be important because we were in the basilica itself, not in one of the many side chapels, and a large number of cardinals and bishops were participating.

In the candle-lit basilica, Michelangelo's flawlessly proportioned design lent itself to this ethereal setting of sanctity. Although there must have been hundreds of people in the basilica, it did not feel crowded. I recalled the several times that Peter and I had walked from the entrance to the high altar and observed the floor markings that listed the lengths of Canterbury Cathedral, Notre Dame Cathedral, the Cathedral of the Immaculate Conception and other great architectural wonders, each of which could fit easily within St. Peters. I could hardly take in the length and breadth of this perfectly balanced design of the largest church in all of Christendom. At each side chapel pilgrims knelt to pray. I felt a sense of corporate worship and prayer, yet the importance and unique footprint of each individual human person.

As we left the cathedral after the Mass, others in our group told Peter that they were thrilled that he had been selected to be one of the principle con-celebrants.

"I don't have a clue about that. I'm sure it was all a mistake."

"Why do you think it was a mistake?" someone asked.

"For one thing, I can't speak a word of Italian. I think Father Tam got me into this. Where is he?" He looked around. "I haven't seen him since we left the sacristy."

"He said he had to get back to the College."

"I had no idea what I was supposed to do. Father Tam said to just follow the other priests, so that's what I tried to do. I was really afraid I would make a bad mistake and draw attention to myself. I was so relieved when the Mass ended. Then they started lining up for the procession which again, I knew nothing about or why I was in it."

"I was so proud of you," I said. "It was incredible to see you in this great cathedral. Imagine, a married American priest being given this privilege."

"You *would* think that, Mary, only because you didn't have to deal with the problem of what to do."

"I took lots of pictures."

"I'm sure you did. Hmmmm."

I looked at Peter and saw that his smile was more of a grimace. It was not the first time that my enthusiasm for his priesthood had annoyed him. Still, I couldn't help it; it was an honor for him and exciting for all of us from Tulsa.

I thought of him walking in procession in the shadows of the candle-lit basilica. I felt honored to share this moment of personal history and think of our children and grandchildren and the stories we would share about the time their father and grandfather assisted at high Mass in the greatest cathedral in the world.

-11-

When we had been at Holy Family for a time, Peter asked Father Gray and Bishop Beltran for permission to celebrate a healing Mass at five o'clock each Wednesday in the cathedral chapel. The Mass would not be charismatic as healing services often are, but a Mass at which he would administer the sacrament of reconciliation, anointing with holy oil and the laying on of hands. When the Bishop and Father Gray agreed that it would be a good thing, Peter talked to those he thought might be interested and scheduled the first Mass within weeks.

The healing Mass drew an assortment of people: the wise and noteworthy, the humble, even those on the fringes of our society. Among them were those whom God had healed in astonishing circumstances, those who prayed that He would bless them with either physical or spiritual healing or both, and those who came to pray for others.

One person was a homeless man, less than five feet tall with long hair and an untidy beard who called himself Little Peter.

He first brought attention to himself by carrying with him an empty one-gallon plastic milk bottle that he filled with water from the drinking fountain in the hall. Some of the attendees brought him food and clothing and once collected enough money to buy him a warm coat. A week later, he returned, still wearing his old ragged coat, explaining that he had given the new one to a friend who had none.

It was at these weekly Masses that we met Ted and his wife Eileen, who was in the first stages of Alzheimer's disease. To see the two of them week after week, sharing their lives as husband and wife, his devotion to her, and her adoring gaze in return, was an example of the sacredness of Holy Matrimony and life-long union. We watched Eileen slowly progress into the final stages of the disease when she required nursing home care. From that time until her death, Peter accompanied Ted to the nursing home once a month to give Eileen Holy Communion and anoint her. Then he and Ted went to lunch together where Ted was able to share the grief of the loss of his spouse to this tragic disease.

Peter also blessed their marriage at their fiftieth wedding anniversary celebration in the nursing home where Eileen was a patient. I wondered if Eileen was fully aware of the reason for the party, but her eyes sparkled and a girlish smile played on her lips all afternoon. She must have known somewhere inside that the party was in her honor. Ted's love for Eileen was an inspiration to everyone who knew them.

When I think of this loving couple, I am reminded that life is incredibly fragile and that every moment rests in God's loving hands. We cannot know what tomorrow will bring. We know only that God will be there to walk with us.

Peter learned that Bishop William Cox, retired bishop of the Episcopal Diocese of Oklahoma, was a member of the International Order of St. Luke and very much involved in that healing ministry. With Bishop Beltran and Father Gray's permission, he contacted Bishop Cox and invited him to speak at one of the Masses and to the group afterward.

Bishop Cox remained in the congregation during the Mass, a gesture of discretion and courtesy toward Roman Catholics. When the Mass was over, he came forward and received the laying on of hands from Peter. He then turned, gesturing to Peter to kneel, and he placed his hands on Peter's head, blessing his ministry and praying for healing in his life.

As I watched these two men of God, all the years since 1980 and our decision to leave the Episcopal Church flashed through my mind. The hardness of our own Episcopal bishop. The passive unresponsiveness of the archbishop of Seattle. The warmth and welcome we received from Bishop Beltran and many priests and sisters in Tulsa. The censure by others. And now this remarkable love and humility in Bishop Cox.

As I saw him kneeling before Peter, a former Episcopal priest, now a Roman Catholic, the Bishop's openness, his modesty, his grace and the peace he brought to all those present enveloped me in a new reality. I saw here, not only the symbolic truth of the ministry of healing, but the beliefs and framework of discipline and Biblical study that supported the common ministries of these two men in the Episcopal and the Roman Catholic Churches.

It was as though time stood still for those few minutes of spiritual encounter as the breath of the Holy Spirit re-created and refreshed me. Somehow, all the wrongs, the petty differences and squabbles between Christians fell away, meaningless in the shadow of Peter, my husband, a former Episcopal priest and this Episcopal bishop, William Cox, who disregarded liturgical custom to kneel and ask for Peter's blessing. Father and son, brothers in Christ. God's grace touched me deeply in that moment, healing in me the anger and sadness of those years of leaving and becoming.

When one is released from years of anger and resentment, it is an intensely emotional experience. However, more than emotion, my freedom was a fact. God healed me as surely as a boil is lanced and the poison released. I could forgive the man who was our Episcopal bishop for his rude arrogance when we became Catholics. I could forgive the archbishop of Seattle for his insensitive and misguided submission to political correctness. I could forgive errant priests their lack of kindness toward my husband, their brother priest, and me. I was freed from them and all they represented in my past life. I felt strengthened in my gratitude for the gifts I had received in the Episcopal Church—the place where my faith first took root and began to grow.

God reveals Himself to us in many forms. He sent us a homeless man of no particular consequence to anyone. We could have crossed to the "other side of the road" and ignored him. Yet, he gave us an opportunity for caring without any thought of reward or prestige. He sent us an Alzheimer's patient whose devoted husband shared with us their heart-rending journey and their remarkable example of fidelity and trust. He sent us a bishop who himself became forgiveness and reconciliation, and he gave us each other with all our warts and scars.

-12-

As Christmas drew near, Peter's schedule filled up and our times together were fewer and shorter. It became clear that none of our four children would be coming to Tulsa for the holidays. The cost of plane tickets was too great a burden for them or us. Once again, Christmas found me feeling isolated and sad as I anticipated that we would be alone.

I recalled 1983, our painful first Christmas in Tulsa. Peter and I were alone with no possible way to be with our family. It was the first time I had been separated from any of the children at Christmas. To make things worse, we did not feel secure about our place in the Pastoral Provision program.

By that time, it was clear that the priest in the parish where we had been assigned, did not support us and was already attempting to have Bishop Beltran remove us. That Christmas was one of our lowest periods since we had left the Episcopal Church.

I remember how, at that Christmas Eve Mass I could not stop the tears from running down my face. I looked toward the altar and watched my husband herded around the sanctuary with obvious impatience and belittling intolerance by the pastor with the entire congregation looking on. If I saw it, surely others could see it too. In disbelief, infuriated and deeply hurt, I knelt transfixed. The priest's behavior was juvenile and bizarre. The tears streamed down my face. I felt embarrassed and ashamed that I had become so spectacularly unglued.

As the church emptied at the end of the Mass and I continued in my kneeling position with my head bowed, I could only dimly hope that those sitting near me had been so filled with the magic of Christmas that they would attribute my quiet hysteria to some sort of religious fervor.

All four children were in college and we had little money for gifts. I will never know what I had in mind when I sent each of the children three pairs of underpants and a New Testament Bible for Christmas.

One consolation: it has been an endless source of merciless teasing ever since.

The holidays in Tulsa had been a difficult time for me from the beginning and as our second Christmas at Holy Family Cathedral approached, I vowed I would change things. While my husband was busy serving others, I would make a place for myself by finding a way to give something back to the people around me who had given me so much.

Holy Family Cathedral was a downtown parish attended by people from all over the city and surrounding suburbs. A few elderly, low-income folks lived in the rundown apartment buildings in the adjoining blocks. One day after the noon Mass as Peter and I crossed the cathedral parking lot to our car I looked across the street to the shabby buildings with their narrow dingy windows.

"Do you know anything about the people who live there?" I asked Peter, gesturing toward the apartments.

"They're older folks living on social security checks. They are mostly alone. No family in Tulsa. Some forgotten. They live near the cathedral so they can walk to Mass," he said, opening the car door for me.

"Do they come to Christmas Masses? Or, do they seem to leave town? Maybe to be with children?"

"No, I don't think most of them have children they can go to. Why do you ask?"

"I think I'd like to do something for them."

"Oh?"

"You know how hard it is for me at Christmas without the kids?"

"Yes?"

"After the holidays last year I vowed I'd never sit around and feel sorry for myself again."

"Good."

"Well, I think I'd like to have a Christmas dinner in the Green Room at the cathedral. I could invite people who may have nowhere else to go." I turned toward him in the car, waiting for his response.

"I don't know if they would come. They're shy and keep to themselves. One little lady always sits in the corner of the back pew. I noticed that she was always alone and left Mass without shaking my hand, so one day I stopped her before she had a chance to leave. Now, she stops and greets me and she nearly always asks about you." He turned to me and smiled. "She told me that she has been coming to the cathedral all her life, and I am the first priest to call her by name. I think her son may have been a priest who later left to marry."

"I've thought about whether they would come or not," I said, thinking of the people I wanted to reach. "I'd want to mail invitations to them and then follow up with a telephone call a few days before Christmas. If they need transportation, I'll get volunteers to pick them up. It doesn't really matter how many we have. If we start with only three or four people, I'll feel that we've begun something worthwhile."

"I know you could cook the dinner, but how would you pay for it?" Peter asked.

"I thought I could ask Father Gray to pay for the turkey and maybe the cathedral Women's Club would donate some funds to help out. I think I could probably get food donations too. I could bring candles and things from home to decorate."

"Sounds like a good idea. Go ahead and do it."

"I'll talk to Father Gray and see what he thinks," I said as we pulled into our driveway. Now I needed to start thinking about our own dinner before Peter had to leave for a meeting at the cathedral.

I was delighted when nearly everyone I talked to expressed enthusiasm and wanted to be a part of the Christmas dinner.

That first year we had four people attend. In fact, there were nearly twice as many workers as guests, but that didn't discourage us. We had games and prizes and carried out our plans to make the day special for those who had no family with whom to share it. Everyone ended the day feeling warm-hearted and fulfilled. Important to me, I experienced a personal victory. Through my own creativity and determination, I overcame the loneliness that so easily enveloped me. I had made friends at Holy Family with people who accepted me as a woman and as Father Peter's wife. I had touched their lives and they had touched mine. Together, we were learning who I was among them. I felt that it was a new beginning, at the very least a new chapter, not only in my own personal journey but also in my relationship to the people as their priest's wife.

The following Christmas, the Cathedral Knights of Columbus, a group that Peter had been instrumental in establishing, offered to help. Our attendance tripled. This time guests and workers were equal in number.

The third year the Green Room was full of partygoers and helpers, more than sixty people altogether. Everyone entered into the spirit of the season with games and prizes and more food than we could possibly eat. We took the extra food to Catholic Charities for the homeless.

The Holy Family Christmas, now sponsored by the Knights of Columbus, continues to be an annual event looked forward to by everyone. Through the men and women who carry on this parish ministry, I feel honored and validated.

Holy Family Christmas part kitchen helpers

-13-

"Father Dally?"

"Yes."

It was a priest from St. Gregory's College in Shawnee. "Father, our graduating class has selected you for their baccalaureate speaker this year. Would you be willing to come?"

"I would be honored. Have you run this by Archbishop Salatka?"

"I don't understand. Why would I need to do that?"

"I'm a married priest. I would not want to come into the diocese without the Archbishop's permission."

"Well, yes but...well, I can't imagine that he won't approve."

"I think you should run it by him."

"Well, okay, if you think it's wise."

A day or two later Peter received a phone call from a man who was a member of the Scottish Rite Masons in Tulsa.

"Our Tulsa lodge traditionally has a dinner on Holy Thursday in celebration of the Last Supper. We always invite a minister to be our speaker. However, we have never had a Catholic priest. Would you consider speaking to us this year?"

"Yes, I could do that, but I'll need to get permission from Bishop Beltran. I'll let you know in a couple of days."

When Peter talked to Bishop Beltran, he was pleased to have a priest from our diocese invited to speak at St. Gregory College. Bishop was amused that a Catholic priest had been invited to speak to the Masonic organization and said, "Sure you can speak to them, if you don't embarrass me." He smiled.

About a week after Peter received the two invitations, he had another phone call from the monk at St. Gregory College.

"Father Peter, I talked with Archbishop Salatka and he will not give permission for you to come into the Archdiocese. I am truly sorry, and I might add, very embarrassed."

"I was afraid he might feel that way."

"I can't tell you how disappointed I am. Moreover, the students requested you and I know they will be disappointed."

The next day Peter saw Bishop Beltran in the cathedral rectory.

"Bishop, I won't be speaking at St. Gregory's."

"Oh? Why is that?"

"Archbishop Salatka doesn't want a married priest in his diocese."

"Oh..." Bishop Beltran's face froze.

"It's okay." Peter laughed nervously.

"I'm so sorry this happened to you, Father Peter. I had no idea."

On Holy Thursday evening, I went with Peter to the Scottish Rite Temple where he talked to a non-Catholic organization that some might even say is anti-Catholic. This was Tulsa, the "buckle of the Bible belt", where Baptists and other fundamentalists make up the majority of Christians. It felt strange to be welcomed by non-Catholics in this region of our country where the Ku Klux Klan had historically singled out and persecuted Catholics, some say as frequently as they had Blacks and Jews. It felt especially strange since Peter had not been allowed to speak in the Archdiocese of Oklahoma City by our own church.

Once again it seemed peculiar that an Archbishop, or any Catholic for that matter, would not recognize a validly ordained Catholic priest because he was married. However, I thought it likely the Archbishop would give a reason other than our marriage to justify his decision as that is what usually occurred in these situations.

When we entered the Pastoral Provision, we had thought and expected that any program put forth by the Holy Father would automatically be recognized and accepted by all Catholics, particularly those in leadership positions. While our early experiences with the hierarchy in Seattle proved otherwise, we were shocked and dismayed to find that this archbishop, with whom our own bishop worked closely, did not recognize the Holy Father's program of the Pastoral Provision and a married man's priesthood.

To say that priesthood rests on a celibate lifestyle limits the giftedness that is intrinsic in holy orders. Celibacy is not a doctrine of the Catholic Church. It is not Christian theology. It is a rule, and it can be changed with the stroke of a pen, just as the Holy Father had done for the men in the Pastoral Provision.

Was I angry? Of course I felt angry. It seemed that each time we began to feel comfortable in this new ministry something unexpected would crop up, reducing any sense of real normalcy.

"Do you remember how you didn't want me working here the first time Bishop Beltran assigned me to Holy Family?" Peter, smiling, asked Father Gray one day when they were having coffee.

Father Gray laughed. "No, that can't be true. You were never assigned here."

"I came the second Sunday after my ordination for the five o'clock Mass and you said you didn't need me any more. I think that Father McClellan was going to be able to come back or something."

"I don't remember that at all."

"I think Mary may still have the letter from Bishop Beltran assigning me here when I was ordained."

"I'd like to see that. I—I can't believe I'd do such a thing."

"I'll bring the letter." As he started to leave the room, Peter turned back. "It's okay, George. I'm here now and sometimes things happen for a good reason. By the way, I respect you and I enjoy our ministry together immensely."

When Peter told me about this conversation, I produced the letter and a copy of the Eastern Oklahoma Catholic listing the priest's assignments in 1985. When he gave them to Father Gray, he was clearly surprised. He had forgotten the incident entirely, and could not imagine why he had told Peter he did not want him there.

When taken in context of the sad things that had happened to us on this journey, the reader might ask if I believed Father Gray.

Yes, I believed him. We had come to know him as a priest of integrity. Clearly, ours was a difficult situation for him to accept. We had grown fond of Father Gray and he deeply appreciated Peter's ministry. Early in our present relationship, we had set past difficulties aside as unimportant and happening a long time ago.

-14-

Sacred Heart Catholic Church

Skiatook, Oklahoma

1991

In the spring of 1991, when we had been at the cathedral for four years, Bishop Beltran called Peter to his office again. Bishop wanted him to take two parishes: St. William Church in Skiatook fourteen miles north of Tulsa and St. Jude Church in north Tulsa. He would be the administrator in both parishes.

When he came home, Peter told me about the meeting. "I had thought we would be at Holy Family until I retire," he said. "By the way, it's pronounced with the accent on the first syllable: Ski-a-took. The first syllable is pronounced *sky* and the *a* is soft. He demonstrated for me. "Ski-a-took. That's the best I can do. The local folks put an Okie twang on it. I just can't say it the way they do." We both laughed.

"What does it mean?"

"I have no idea but I'm sure we'll find out."

"What a surprise. We haven't even heard rumors." I laughed again.

"I didn't tell you, but I happened to see Father Angelo last week and he congratulated me on my new assignment."

"Not again?"

Since coming to the diocese, each time that Peter's assignments were changed by Bishop Beltran, we had heard rumors from various priests days and sometimes weeks before the Bishop called him to his office to tell him. The Catholic grapevine was rooted in fertile soil and well tended in Tulsa. It had made us uncomfortable early on, but we had come to enjoy this amusing anomaly, which seemed especially ironic in this Roman Catholic culture of concealment.

"Of course, I'm very happy that we'll have our own parish. I won't be the pastor you know."

"I don't understand."

"Under the conditions of the Pastoral Provision no married priest may be the pastor of a parish."

"But I thought when you were assigned to Holy Family that was resolved."

"Not really. The official word on the matter is that a parish ministry for a married man would be scandalous to the laity." Peter used the Latin phrase and laughed.

"The only scandal is the rejection by some bishops and priests and the fact that you are given what some might consider a lower status simply because you are married. It's a stupid rule. If you're pastor, you're pastor."

"I know, Mary, but this is the way Rome does it. You know that it won't make one bit of difference in how my ministry is regarded by Bishop Beltran. My title will be administrator, but I'll be the pastor in every way. Bishop knows it's an unfair rule."

"One more thing to explain..." I sighed.

"Most won't know the difference or even care, and those who do will think it's stupid, of course."

"Why do they make such a fuss about a married priest costing more money than a celibate? It simply isn't true. Catholic priests are better compensated than many married protestant ministers. When you realize that a Catholic priest lives in a furnished rectory, gets a food allowance and in larger parishes, a housekeeper and cook, auto expenses, medical and dental insurance and retirement benefits, plus his stipend for personal expenses like clothing and vacation, it is a very good living. Are priests allowed to keep their Mass stipends and wedding and funeral fees too?"

"I think that's optional. They may keep fees or gifts for personal use or they can turn them over to the parish general fund or some special need. It's really left up to the individual priest."

"I wonder what it will be like for us alone in a parish," I mused.

"Bishop Beltran said he wants this to be my last. He wants me to be there until I retire."

"That's wonderful."

"I told the Bishop that I want to be treated like the celibate priests."

"You mean sleep in separate bedrooms?"

"Very funny." He smiled. "No, I mean get the same stipend and benefits. They need to realize that a married priest can manage well in a parish ministry without causing additional expense."

"I'm really glad you did that. They have no idea how tough it is for Protestant ministers to manage on their small earnings."

"I'll get a smaller stipend. Do you think it will make much of a difference?"

"Not at all. I knew where every penny went when we were in the Episcopal Church. I was lucky if we had five dollars left at the end of the month."

"The kids always said you put together the best meals when there seemed to be nothing in the house to cook."

I thought of the hamburger gravy and mashed potatoes, creamed tuna served over baking powder biscuits and the Poor Boy cookies. I made the cookies with water and they didn't contain eggs. They consisted of lots of sugar, flour, and cheap margarine. Oh, and a few raisins. The kids loved them. They had little nutritional value, but I could always find the makings for Poor Boy cookies.

"There was something really good about those days," I said.

"Yes, but they were hard too."

"I wouldn't want to go back. Still, sometimes the hardest times are the happiest. My mother said that the best years of her life were the depression years when the family could barely put food on the table and she sewed school dresses out of printed flour sacks for my sisters."

"My family had lean times too."

"I'm delighted we'll be living in a parish again—and I'm so glad you'll be on your own. I love being with the people. I've loved every minute at Holy Family."

"Yes—well, there's just one thing you should know."

"What's that?" I felt a dampening of my spirits.

"I had a call from Father Neal Brogan. He congratulated me, but said they are not doing us any favors. He says Bishop Beltran is sending me there because he can't get anyone else to take it. Apparently, there is a lot of fighting and bickering in the parish. Neal said that some of the people left and went over to St. Teresa's in Collinsville during the time he was priest there."

In the following days, other priests came to Peter one by one with similar stories.

The current pastor, who would be transferred from Skiatook to Okmulgee was equally cautious. "You'll need to be careful. People are starting to come back," he said. "But the money is short. I told Bishop Beltran that I don't think they can support a married man. They didn't do so well with me."

"We'll make it work," Peter said.

Shortly before Peter learned from the Bishop of his new assignment, I left my job at Bishop Kelley High School and took a new position at Oklahoma State University College of Osteopathic Medicine (OSU-COM). I felt saddened to leave my job with a Catholic high school, but the salary I received there was minimal with inadequate retirement benefits. With only ten years until I retired, I determined that I needed to move to a position with a good salary and retirement benefits. OSU-COM offered that opportunity.

When the Cathedral Women's Club learned that we had been assigned to Skiatook, they were delighted for Peter and insisted that they help me pack. As I went about the house organizing our things, I thought of our leaving Vashon Island eight years before. I recalled how difficult it was to peel away the flotsam and jetsam of nineteen years of raising children in one community.

Although our children were young adults when we left the Island, I had saved many of their childhood toys and keep-sakes, expecting that their children would have them someday. However, it was not possible to take them with us to Oklahoma.

It was painful for me to let go of things like the chalet dollhouse and furniture that Peter and our friend, Tommy Tomlinson, had made for Monica and Tess. I wondered what I might do with the lead soldiers that John and Kurt had spent hours molding and painting in authentic detail with their dad. Our attic had been full of treasures for the family to make decisions about. I hadn't wanted to do it alone. Worse, all four children were in denial that anything about our lives was going to change. They avoided talking about these things over the telephone. Nor would they come home to help me decide what to do with them. The stuff of our lives on the Island, these things were connected to all of us through the memories of the growing years they represented. I wondered how the things of a lifetime could mean so little to our children. I told myself they were occupied with college and friends. Still, I could not deny that the children resented the fact that Peter and I were moving to another part of the country, that home was leaving them. It was painful for me to realize that the things that meant so much to me meant little to them, at least at that time in their lives.

Now, in Tulsa, eight years later, thinking about the previous move from Vashon Island, I realized that I faced many of the same challenges. As I wrapped china and glassware, I conceded that this too was a big change. We would be on our own again in a parish and living in a rectory and I would miss my children more than ever. They were happy for us. They knew what having his own parish meant to their dad. I could only hope that this might mean more holidays together, that they would come once again to their dad's church, that we could resume a semblance of family life, at least during their visits.

I can say now that for years I dreamed of these possibilities and slowly, as time passed, I began to understand that as we grow and move on to new vistas, though we reminisce and dream of past times, those days are gone forever and live only in our hearts. Life is a journey, ever changing, ever awakening us to grow, to leave the past, and to remember those years with love and gratitude. Finally, to move into the present and the rich promise it alone offers.

-15-

One day in the midst of packing, Peter asked, "Want to drive out to Skiatook? We could see the church and rectory."

"I'd like that."

We drove through the streets of north Tulsa past St. Jude, the mission church that Peter would also serve. From there we headed out Peoria Avenue and State Highway 11, which took us into Skiatook.

We were quiet as we drove north and I recalled a similar drive years before when I saw this town for the first time. It was 1984 and spring rains had deluged Eastern Oklahoma. Bird Creek, skirting the eastern boundary of Skiatook had flooded its banks covering Highway 11 to the south, and cutting the town off from the east on Highway 20.

The water on "11" had receded enough to allow traffic into the town. Mud was everywhere in the three block radius fronting it. The houses in this older, poorer part of town appeared to be sinking in the debris that had washed down Bird Creek and over its banks to find its resting place in yards and against dwellings. Here and there, owners had wisely built their houses on elevated foundations or stilts. In John Zink Park, we spotted the soccer goal posts and baseball backstops, but the park was completely submerged.

"Yuk! I hope I never have to live here," I had said.

"I don't think you'll have to worry. I'll never be assigned to a parish."

That was in 1984.

Now, in 1991 we were about to move to Skiatook to live in the same neighborhood. Friends warned that Skiatook lay along what locals call tornado alley. I could not help but wonder if the rectory was subject to rising water as well as tornadoes. It seemed the two might go together.

That day, in this new advent of our lives, the sun was shining and the roads were clear. We drove down Rogers Boulevard, the main street, and turned onto Osage Avenue. The church was located at 5th and Osage in the older part of town. Pretty close to the flood plain, I observed, but I kept this to myself.

The church itself was a traditional rectangular building made of grey Osage rock. The porch, supported by four tall wooden pillars, extended across the front of the building.

In front of the church on a broken and cracked concrete apron stood a statue of the Sacred Heart of Jesus surrounded by a large concrete planter box that grew mostly weeds.

"Wait a minute. Sacred Heart? This is St. William Church." Peter shook his head. "That's strange."

I laughed. "I wonder what that's all about," knowing that every congregation has its own personality and remembering the comments that this was a difficult parish.

We stopped at the rectory but did not find the pastor at home. The church was unlocked so we went inside. I don't remember very much about that first view of our new parish except that I observed three different colors and types of carpet loosely pieced together to cover the floor. Peter noted that the church did not have a confessional, and that the balcony normally used for seating was full of ladders, paint cans, and dusty boxes labeled teen dance decorations and Christmas pageant.

Clearly, it was a poor little church in need of love and attention.

Like two children, we were thrilled.

This was our life: called to ministry in the Catholic Church. Bishop Beltran's confidence in Peter validated our life together both now and in past years in the Episcopal Church.

The responsibility of our own parish would mean greater demands and challenges for me personally. Most of all it would mean the opportunity to more closely examine the role of priest's wife in the Roman Catholic Church.

I had tried to maintain my independence throughout our ministry, and I was determined now to continue that freedom to define and shape my place beside my husband. I was a homemaker, not a theologian, teacher, or musician. Undeniably distaff. I loved participating in parish life but I did not accept leadership roles normally held by laypersons. I would be busy enough with a rectory to care for. There would be meals to prepare for who-knew-how-many and on numerous occasions. Though I was more than satisfied with the number of years I'd already presided over a vicarage or rectory, I could not deny that I delighted in the prospect of this newest challenge. I felt strongly that this was an innovative opportunity for the Church as well.

In the Catholic Church, it seemed that the primary concern regarding the practicality of the married priesthood was the question of money. However, I felt that this was a conclusion arrived at without thorough research and examination of actual celibate priests' expenses as compared to those of a family. Many believed that a congregation, regardless of size, could not afford a married priest. I felt a proper trial would prove otherwise. The Diocese of Tulsa had paid our three married priests a stipend that took into account a family, medical insurance, car reimbursement, and a housing allowance. In Skiatook we would live in the rectory, not requiring a housing allowance.

From the beginning, we had wanted to serve the Catholic Church in the most effective way. At Peter's request, Bishop Beltran gave permission for us to accept the same stipend and benefits as any other priest in the Diocese. Peter discussed it with the Chancellor of the diocese, and asked him to have the accounting office set it up. I would use my salary for my work expenses, which included clothing and a car to commute daily to Tulsa, and place the remainder in savings for our retirement. We wanted to demonstrate that a married priest would not be a financial drain on a congregation. The Chancellor agreed to let us try this as an experiment for an unspecified period.

As far as I was concerned, it was their experiment, not ours. I knew it would work. Catholic priests and people have no perception of the true generosity of their church.

Our personal economic health in the Catholic Church was in striking contrast to the financial challenges we encountered as Episcopalians. Peter had been a high churchman. Consequently, we had served small mission churches. His stipend had been at the low end of the diocesan salary schedule whereas every priest in a Catholic diocese receives the same stipend. I knew how to stretch a dollar and I hoped to dispel the myth that the Catholic Church could not afford married priests.

The future promised an exciting lifestyle and we looked forward to giving back to Bishop Beltran and the Diocese of Tulsa something of their generosity and confidence in us. Eight years earlier, they had welcomed us with our assurance that we would serve the Church to the best of our abilities. This moment had placed us on the crest of the wave, exactly the place where we wanted to be. Indeed, the place to which we believed God had called us.

Years would pass before I accepted the fact that the "expense" of married priests' has little to do with whether the Church would allow priests to marry. It was simply an excuse.

-16-

We took our vacation to the West Coast in May before we moved, because Peter did not feel that we should leave the parish in mid-summer so soon after our arrival.

"How long has it been since we've been to the coast in the spring?" Peter asked as we settled into our seats aboard the American Airlines plane leaving Tulsa.

"Oh, years," I said. "I'd love to see the wild iris in bloom again—and some early rhododendrons and azaleas too."

The native plants whose blooms dotted the roadsides and woodlands in May and early June were among my most cherished memories growing up in coastal Port Orford, Oregon. The Pacific Ocean beaches, Garrison Lake, the Sixes and Elk Rivers' pristine beauty of the 1950s lingered in my blood. Our return each summer to these places had become an annual event that I found I anticipated and planned for, months in advance. This year I would especially treasure a week in our friends' cabin on Sixes Ranch in this beautiful springtime.

"The lambs. I almost forgot that there will be new lambs on the ranch." I smiled.

"A week hardly seems long enough to soak it all in," Peter said.

"I know."

It was a breezy sunny day when we drove down Airport Road and turned off onto the single lane gravel entrance to the Sixes Ranch. As we rounded the curve of the hill, the woods opened up to the panorama below. We drove on around the ridge and down into the basin that formed the mouth of the Sixes River. There were patches of sheep gathered everywhere on the river bottom.

As the valley opened below us on our left, the hill rose on the right. Scrub alder grew near the road. Rare white Port Orford cedar covered the hillsides. Below us, we watched the meandering Sixes River form the southern boundary of the ranch before it yielded to the dunes and the power of the Pacific Ocean. This was the river bottomland, besieged by seasonal rampages and sculpted into the ranch's fertile grazing plateau for the sheep and horses. Cloaked in finely woven new spring grass, the fields and hillsides festooned with clumps of wild iris created a scene of tranquility and calm so reminiscent of the river's name: Sixes, an Indian word thought to mean peace when I grew up here in the fifties. Later I learned that the river is actually named for the Siksestunne Band of the Quoh-to-mah Indians who lived at the mouth of the Sixes near the place where the cabin now stands. However, I liked to think that the river's name meant peace. It fit this place that meant so much to us.

"There's your wild iris," Peter said.

"Isn't it all just too unbelievably beautiful?"

"Yes..."

On past the ranch house, the road rutted still more deeply. At the crest of a rise, the cabin came into view, first marked by a thin trail of smoke coming from the chimney. Our host, Piercy Sweet had built a fire in the wood stove to take away the dampness that permeated coastal homes year round. So different from Oklahoma. Beyond the cabin, we saw the place where the river and the sea meet, the progress slowed only by the enormous Castle Rock a few hundred feet beyond the river's opening to the sea.

"The first time I came here I was only twenty-six years old," Peter mused. "Muriel and Piercy lived on the ranch then. Later when they moved to Bandon, Muriel and the children would come summers and camp near the mouth of the river. I celebrated the Eucharist for them right out there underneath that tree." Peter pointed to the tall fir tree on the grassy riverbank. "When did we start coming here with our family?"

"It was the summer after my dad died, 1970 that would be," I said.

Our children knew this place as a refuge of peace and easy family gatherings, I thought. Soon, our grandchildren would feel it as well. I wondered if Muriel and Piercy could ever know how this tranquil oasis had affected our lives and the way in which our children and we knew each other.

That spring Peter and I read our favorite books and played dominoes. He wrote icons on the sunny porch. We ate fresh salmon and cod. In the afternoons, we hiked through the hillside woods and along the beach, climbing over logs and rocks, savoring the sound of the wind caressing the beach pines. I lugged my cameras and tripods, giving in occasionally to Peter's insistence that he carry them for me. We had Sunday Mass with our life-long friend Father Walter Parker and suppers with my brother and his family.

Father Peter writing Icons on the back porch at the Sixes Ranch cabin.

Then these cool days of warm memories, past and newly made, were over and we were on our way home to Oklahoma. Our thoughts were on the coming weeks when we would leave Holy Family Cathedral a large city parish, and move to Skiatook, a small country parish of about 200 souls, where for the first time, we would be on our own in the Catholic Church.

-17-

The time seemed short to accomplish all that we needed to do to be ready for this transition. "I hate good-byes. Even when we're only moving a few miles away," I said.

"It's good to make a physical break."

I sighed. "I know, but I'd like to see our friends in the city from time to time." The Catholic Diocese of Tulsa was like a big family. We all felt connected across parish boundaries. One could attend Mass in almost any part of the Diocese and find friends and familiar faces.

"There's a saying that is true in both the Episcopal and Catholic Church: priests come and go but the people go on forever," Peter said.

"Um-hmm. I don't think I've ever been actually happy to leave a congregation. Still, it is exciting to look forward to new opportunities and challenges. It's a lot of fun for sure."

"You're right about that."

I could acknowledge that most of the time I embrace a clerical shift in residence. Although it means leaving what I love, it brings with it new friendships. Our life story isn't merely experiences, but attitudes that mold and shape the moments that touch our lives and the lives of those around us. In spite of the sadness I felt about leaving my friends in Tulsa, I looked forward to the many opportunities and challenges ahead for me. Peter and I had loved the people at Holy Family Cathedral for the four years we served there. They dwell in our hearts now. They will forever be a part of our lives.

The Women's Club and the Knights of Columbus at Holy Family held a reception in our honor. The congregation gave us a wonderful send-off as a way of thanking Peter for his ministry and wishing us well in Skiatook. They were as excited as we were about our new parish ministry.

The rectory in Skiatook would be yet another home for the beautiful antique cherry and mahogany pieces that had traveled the plains from Illinois to California with Emma and George Dally, then from rectory to rectory in Washington State and east again with us when we moved to Oklahoma. The ornate chests of drawers seemed immune to the disfiguring of countless moves, both long and short distances, imbued with the patina of many hands—those of children whose hands were still moist from evening clean-ups and those other hands, spotted and wrinkled, calloused and loving.

These familiar furnishings, along with Peter's books and some household and personal items and clothing, could have been easily stored in an ordinary bedroom when we arrived in Tulsa in 1983. In eight years, we had accumulated living room furniture, two desks, a computer, dishes, cooking utensils and more books.

Friends and parishioners offered their strong backs and muscles to move us. One of the permanent deacons who worked for a trucking firm generously provided a truck. It was a beautiful day with excitement in the air as our friends loaded up our things in Tulsa and unloaded them again in Skiatook.

In our new rectory, there was work to do. In the back of the dining room closet, I discovered Christmas cards postmarked twenty-eight years earlier, dishes wrapped in newspapers from the sixties, and Sunday school materials long outdated. The closets smelled of musty newsprint, old mimeograph ink, and dust, but moreover, they held memories of past lives, priests and people, in this small country parish.

Shelves and kitchen cabinets needed washing and sorting through. There was painting, cleaning and shampooing the wall-to-wall carpet throughout the house. It took days just to get the place ready to settle into. I knew this was going to be a house I would love. It felt like home from the first day.

Since there would now be a woman in the rectory, the people had planned to remodel the kitchen, expecting to have it finished before our arrival. However, a month earlier, a tornado had ripped through Skiatook destroying more than forty-five homes and damaging others. Contractors and carpenters mobilized to take care of these more urgent needs of tornado victims. The rectory remodeling was postponed of necessity.

It seemed that nearly everyone we talked to in those first weeks apologized for the condition of the kitchen. Secretly, I felt relieved that they had not remodeled it. The room was square, as square as a room in a ninety-year-old house could be. It was a great country kitchen, and I liked it just the way it was. With a flat roof and no second floor, the kitchen appeared to be an add-on, though the old-timers told me later that it was a part of the original two-story house. However, it was not more than a few days before I found that this same roof was a magnet for summer heat. Even with central air conditioning, when the outdoor temperature rose above ninety, the room was stifling. We installed a ceiling fan donated by a parishioner. It helped, but the entire time we lived there, summer meals were often cold salads or food that came from Mac's Barbecue and the Super H food store deli. It was simply too hot to cook on the gas stove. However, we found that the heat from the gas range was a blessing in the poorly insulated rectory when the thermometer took a dive in January.

Most of all, I loved the old kitchen cabinets. They were the metal kind from the forties— the same style as in our farm-house when I was a child. They were large, had wide doors and deep shelves that could easily accommodate my largest platters and baking pans. Of course, they were rusty and the paint was chipped and dull. No question, they were an eyesore. The counter tops were linoleum, faded and worn through in places, need-ing to be replaced.

Peter painted the cabinets a bright marine blue and the kitchen walls and ceiling white. A parishioner, J.J. Archer cov-ered the countertops with my choice of white Formica.

I sighed when I opened the pantry and saw the walls. They were full of dry rot. Using it was out of the question. Another parishioner, Vern Jones, relined the shelves with fresh wood inserts making them useful and beautiful. Lastly, the parish replaced the old gas kitchen stove and refrigerator with gleaming new ones.

The country style table and chairs in the center of the kitchen were too large for the room. Nevertheless, it would become a favorite place for a relaxed cup of coffee or iced tea when parishioners stopped by.

I had a sense that this house held many secrets. It was strange to see a trap door in one corner of the kitchen floor. We weren't brave enough to inspect it on our own, but one day when our parishioner, Paul Guilfoyle stopped he explained that it led to a "fraidy" hole. Paul, a tall, lean man, a little bent from arthritis, had his eightieth birthday a few weeks after we arrived. A plainspoken man, his was the heart of small town Oklahoma. We loved him and his wife Gertie from the beginning.

"Now, this is whur y'all go when you hear a tornada warnin," Paul explained. "Don't look out the winder. Don't wait t'see what's goin' to happen. Just git down in this here hole. You won't have time for nothin' else if there's a tornada."

"What's down there?" I asked, doubtful that it was a place I wanted to be.

"Well, the furnace—probly dirt and some little ole spiders."

"What about snakes?" I asked.

"Ohhhh, I don't know. Might be one or two."

"Where do the snakes—the poisonous ones—go when a tornado hits?" Peter asked.

"Oh, they git in ditches or go underground."

"Underground? But, that's where we'll be." I looked to Peter for assurance. "Isn't it?"

"Don't worry, Mary. I'll take care of you."

"I can hardly wait."

God help us if there is a tornado, I thought.

The kitchen, living/dining room and priest's office made up the ground floor of the rectory. There was also a small utility room and a half bath. Peter preferred to have his office away from the rectory, providing confidentiality for anyone coming to see him and privacy for us in our home. We would make the former priest's office into a library for my computer and books.

We took the worn out furniture and office computer out of the living room and moved them to Peter's temporary office in the education building, next door to the rectory.

Then, with the furniture we brought with us, we made the living room into a comfortable sitting room suitable for meetings and other gatherings. I suggested we remove the worn accordion plastic divider that separated the living room from the dining room. With it gone, the room returned to its spacious origins. We were delighted with the results.

The dining room's antique table, chairs, and buffet were solid mahogany. I loved this scarred furniture, knowing it had seen nearly a century of clerical meals and gatherings. The heart of the rectory, the old table held the secrets of life here; baptisms, weddings, funerals, not to mention the achievements, disappointments, and tragedies of both priests and people.

The wide stairway began in the hall by the front door. The carved Victorian banister dramatically spanned the length of the stairway and divided the second floor into two large rooms with a full bathroom in-between.

The walls of the priest's bedroom were solid cedar paneling, not the thin veneer used in newer homes. Two large closets and shelved cabinets took up an entire wall. We were surprised to find that the bedroom was nearly soundproof. Whether on purpose or coincidentally, due to the heavy paneling, we weren't sure. Later, Peter would have his regular Sunday afternoon nap tucked in this quiet cocoon and the world would go on around him. Years later I learned that the paneling in the bedroom had been an effort to create a more masculine environment. The sound proofing had been a bonus, and certainly a blessing for a tired priest.

When we had been in residence for about six weeks, we held an open house so the parish could see how we had arranged the rectory. The people seemed to like the small changes we had made throughout the house. However, there was a noticeable silence when each approached the bedroom, and I wondered if they were embarrassed to contemplate a priest sleeping with a woman. At the very least, they seemed unsure how to react. However, since I had been sleeping with Peter for thirty-four years, I decided not to be concerned. I felt sure that once they knew us, they would feel comfortable with our marriage.

The north window in the bedroom had been carelessly covered when fiberglass siding was installed on the outside of the house ten or so years earlier. On the inside, the window and its frame had never been covered. An unsightly hole in the wall allowed a view of the back of the siding. A large mirror attempted to cover the hole. Not high on our list of priorities, this eyesore remained for our seven-year residency. Since we did not own bedroom furniture, we used the assortment of dressers and nightstands left there by former priests.

"About all we need here is a chain ladder," Peter said, examining the windowsill and clearance to the ground.

"A ladder?"

"In case of fire. I can anchor it right here under the window, so we can just toss it through the window. Then we'll have a way out if there's a fire."

"I think I'd rather jump."

"And break your neck?"

"I don't want to chance anything that's anchored to this old wood in the wall. You saw the dry rot in the kitchen."

"Well, in that case we can just wrap it around the legs of this heavy dresser." He bent down and lifted the end of the dresser. Too easily I thought.

"I still think I'll jump."

The second upstairs room was even larger than the bedroom. A floor to ceiling bookshelf surrounded a bay window that overlooked the church across the street. It was the perfect place for Peter's private study. Here he would write his homilies and have his morning scripture study and meditation. Still another wonderful cedar closet filled an adjacent corner.

At the other end of this large space, I created a private sitting/living room where we could escape the demands of the parish and whatever might be going on downstairs. We arranged two of the rectory recliners, of which there were five in all, (acquired by the former pastor to accommodate Monday night football), and a sofa, some end tables and our favorite books nearby. The large-screen rectory television, whose original purpose had also been Monday night football, remained in the corner.

It was fun to fill the house with our personal possessions—photographs and other family things like great-grandmother's antiques and Peter's paintings, making it our own. I had longed for a home like this since our arrival in Tulsa. Immediately, I loved its warmth and coziness. I predicted that it would be a wonderful house in which to live, and I was right.

-18-

In actuality, that first Sunday in Skiatook held no similarity to the last Sunday of Peter's ministry in the Episcopal Church on Vashon Island. However, many of the same feelings surfaced for me and filled my thoughts as I acknowledged that all that we had hoped and prayed for had become a reality. Without a doubt, it was cause not only for celebration and gratitude, but also for trust in the Holy Spirit for whatever lay ahead. I had no need to turn away from the sweetness of the moment, but in a kind of contradiction, I felt insecure and apprehensive.

I expected our lives to change dramatically in this small rural congregation. With Peter in charge here, he would bear the brunt of any dissatisfaction, and this parish had a reputation for being hard on priests. I dreaded that part.

In addition, Holy Family Cathedral was a downtown parish, and people came from all over the city and suburbs to worship there. While many had lived in Tulsa all their lives, a number also had moved there from other parts of the country. Rarely did folks come to Oklahoma to live in rural areas like Skiatook where services were minimal. The two congregations would be quite different so this would be a new adventure for us involving Midwestern culture and custom. Still, I felt like a new bride and just plain scared when I crossed the street for Mass that first Sunday morning.

Folks in the entry way hushed when I came through the door. They nodded good morning and some offered their hands in greeting, but I don't remember anyone speaking to me. I quickly went to the side aisle and found a seat in what had years ago become my favored place, midway in the church.

Jimmie and Jeannette Qualls sat two rows in front of me. I knew them by sight because they had frequently attended Mass at the cathedral. It was a relief to see folks I knew. A full-blooded Cherokee, Jimmie leaned back, his body half turned toward the seated congregation. His elbow hung lazily over the back of the pew. He chewed gum as he twirled his big black cowboy hat in his free hand.

"Yep, Father Pete's a classic priest," he said loud enough for everyone around him to hear.

I felt the adrenalin rise in my blood. My outward appearance of calm belied the tension I felt inside. I dared not look around me, fearing that if I did, I would bolt from the church. Repeating a simple silent prayer, I quieted, and gradually became aware of other activity around me.

The church buzzed with preparations for the Mass. A guitarist, whom I had noticed wearing cowboy attire, and two or three women practiced bits and pieces of songs with Martha the organist whom I had already met. Altar boys whispered among themselves, then took up the processional cross and candles. Old women smiled and nodded. A boy and girl leaned together, whispered secrets and shared shy smiles.

Peter's confident voice greeted latecomers. "Good morning. Hello there. Haven't I seen you at the cathedral?"

I looked toward the altar. It was the same yet it seemed different. What? The tabernacle within which the Blessed Sacrament was reserved had been on a side table on our first visit here. Now it was on an altar against the wall in the middle of the sanctuary. Had that altar been there before? There was something else too, but I couldn't identify it. All I knew for sure was that the church was buzzing; I could feel the tension around me.

Could this be about me? The priest having a wife? I realized that almost no one had looked in at the rectory during the week. In retrospect, that did seem odd. In the Episcopal parishes where Peter had ministered, people were curious about the new priest and his family. Sometimes they welcomed us with a casserole or pie. It made me feel uneasy, but it might be as simple as their wanting to give us privacy. I sat quietly, looked straight ahead and prayed. After a while, the Mass began.

Then it was over, and the congregation moved to the hall for donuts and coffee. The people were shy with me. Many of them introduced themselves and talked briefly. Still, it seemed an interminable time before the coffee hour ended. Not one person had said anything to me about the physical changes in the church.

When the stragglers had left, Peter and I walked across the parking lot to the rectory, exhausted and grateful for the privacy of our home.

"Now, I know you're mad," Peter said closing the kitchen door.

"No."

"I can tell by the way you..."

"What did you do?" I demanded.

"Well, you know I've had Steve and Joe from the cathedral Knights out here putting in the new confessional."

"Don't change the subject. I mean what did you do in the Church?"

"Well, we put in the confessional, like I said. Then I found the original altar that was in the church before Vatican II. It was in that shack next to the church. I painted it and put it in the sanctuary and placed the tabernacle on it."

"Okay..."

"Then I moved the statues of St. Jude and the Blessed Mother into more prominent places in front. It was out of balance before."

"Yes..."

He took a deep breath. "And I took a saw and cut the cross down."

"You what?"

"It was ugly, Mary. You remember."

"No, I don't," I interrupted him.

"Yes you do. The horizontal bar and the vertical bar were the same length. It was square."

"So?"

"It was awful. Like a swastika."

"You had no right. Do you realize the tension in the church this morning? People didn't like it."

"Now Mary, not one person said anything to me about it."

"That's what I mean. Do you really think they loved it and didn't say anything? I'm surprised they didn't throw things at you."

"They'll get used to it, and then they'll love it. I'm going to take a nap." He turned and left me without further discussion.

That week I attended a Catholic Business and Professional Women's meeting in Tulsa. Friends asked me if Peter and I had settled in and how did we like Skiatook. Before I could answer, someone said, "I heard Father Peter took a chainsaw to the cross." Everyone at the table laughed.

I took a deep breath and after a moment joined in the laughter. I felt compelled to explain, but how could I?

"This is a good argument for celibacy," I said, laughing.

One day the volunteer director of religious education came by. She asked to see how we had arranged the rectory. "Does this mean that the rectory is going to be a home?" she asked.

"Yes," I explained. "Bishop Beltran feels that the church office shouldn't be in the rectory. There's a trend away from that."

"Oh. Well, where will Father have his office?"

"It will be in the education building temporarily. Hopefully he won't be in your way," I laughed. "As soon as the little house on the corner of the property is vacant, he will have the office there."

"Oh, I heard that the renters had been asked to move. It's just as well; they're not paying anyway."

"I imagine some work will have to be done on it before he moves his office there."

"We had remodeled the house so the church would get some income from renters." She looked away. "Oh well, they only actually paid the rent for one or two months." She started to leave, and then turned back to me. "My husband is concerned because Father Peter doesn't want to charge tuition for religious education this year. I don't understand. We've always charged ten dollars per child. We need the money to support the church."

"I don't know anything about that. You'll have to talk to him."

"I thought he would talk to you about it."

"No... I don't get involved in those decisions." I gave her what I hoped was a warm smile. "I'm sure he must have a good reason if that's what he's planning."

It had become clear by this time that this young woman's husband and Peter were at odds. The man seemed to oppose everything Peter suggested; then, he would run to the former pastor, who would encourage him, and then call Peter.

When I asked Peter about the tuition, he explained, "I don't want to charge for our religious education program. I don't want to nickel and dime people. They're already giving to the church through the weekly offering. They shouldn't have to fork over more money because their kids go to Sunday school."

"I agree with that, but maybe you should let it go this first year."

"What's the big deal with these people?" Peter asked. "They balk at every suggestion I make."

"I think this man feels that you're on his turf. It seems to me he's pretty much used to doing whatever he wants. He's very close friends with the last priest."

"Well, I'm not having Monday night football here. I don't even like to watch football."

"Come on now, do you think that has anything to do with it?" I smiled. "Surely not."

"I took his wife through the church when Steve and Joe were putting in the confessional. She looked at it and told me that she had never made a confession in her life." He shook his head. "And *she's* determining what our children will be taught in religious education."

"Oh dear."

"I don't know, but I have the feeling that there's no way I can make them happy."

-19-

We chose the Sunday of Labor Day weekend to have a barbecue for the parish. Many friends came from Tulsa as well. We bought hamburger, hot dogs, and chips. I made salads; the altar society brought desserts. It was going to be a big celebration to kick-off the religious education year.

The evening before the barbecue, I was busy in the rectory kitchen. I noticed that the education director and her husband were working in the education building. About 9 pm, they came to the back door of the rectory. "Is Father here?" she asked. Her husband hung back, standing at the bottom of the porch steps.

"No. He was called out. However, he should be back soon. Is there anything I can help you with?"

"No..." She hesitated and turned to her husband. He nodded for her to go ahead. "Well...could you just give this to him?" she asked, handing me a bulky envelope.

"I'd be glad to," I said. "Won't you come in for a minute? Would you like a cold drink?"

She turned toward her husband who looked away. "No, we best be getting home."

They left without another word.

When Peter came home, he opened the envelope. It contained their keys to the church and a letter of resignation with little explanation: only that they could no longer be involved in the parish because of Peter.

Peter telephoned one of the other teachers to tell her of the resignation and get her advice.

"Well, Father, they called all of the Sunday school teachers and tried to get us to leave with them. We all turned them down. They're leaving this parish and going over to Collinsville."

"I see."

"I wouldn't worry about it, Father. They decided before they met you that they weren't going to like you."

"Hmmm. Well, thanks."

"Talk about dramatics," I said. "Here it is the night before the Sunday school kick-off and the director of religious education leaves the parish. That's a great example of Christian living for our young people."

"Better sooner than later," Peter said.

"Oh, I don't know. I hate to see anybody filled with so much anger that they feel compelled to try to destroy another person, much less the parish."

"If we don't let them, they can't do it."

"Still, it ripples through the congregation like a stone tossed into a pool of water."

Peter yawned. "Well, tomorrow's a big day. We'd better get some sleep."

"Thank God the other teachers aren't going with them."

The parish turned out in full force for the barbecue the next day. The air sizzled with conversation and good feeling while the autumn sun shone and a gentle breeze nudged and cooled the rectory back yard. Children played tag beyond the parked cars. There seemed to be an especially positive air as we moved toward the future together.

Every day I drove to my job in Tulsa. It was a forty-five minute commute in each direction and gave me considerable time to think. In the past, I had found parish squabbles the most difficult aspect of our ministry. I did not mind the demands and schedules or the weekends when I barely had time to eat a relaxed meal, much less read the Sunday paper. I loved the people, but I loved my husband too. I agonized, wishing Peter would slow down and wait for the people to catch up. These thorny times drained the energy and joy right out of me.

I cringed as I thought of how, in my anger and frustration, I had said only days earlier to a Skiatook parishioner, "You folks are known for your fighting and bickering. I'll attend Mass at another parish before I'll sit here and listen to it."

Then, I regretted speaking so openly, knowing it would be repeated throughout the congregation.

In the Catholic Church it is the priest's prerogative to make changes. Whether building a confessional, moving the tabernacle to the center of the sanctuary, redesigning the cross, or not charging fees for Sunday school, the priest may decide. When a priest goes to a new parish, he has two choices: make changes he believes are needed or proceed more slowly. I did not agree with Peter's quick changes but I was not the priest nor was I a layperson in the congregation. Caught in the middle, I could do nothing more than support my husband and hope things would get better.

-20-

I thought of the difficulties and challenges of the years since we became Catholics: some beyond our control due to the rarity of a married man endeavoring to become a Catholic priest and still others the result of our own frailties. Those were complicated days and burdened with pain on many levels. Now in yet another "first", I recalled again one of my favorite Catholic "saints," Father Solanus Casey, a Capuchin monk who lived from 1870-1957. Shortly after we became Catholics, I learned about Father Solanus from our daughter, Monica, which made my fondness for this remarkable man a double blessing. Monica had attended Fort Wright College in Spokane, Washington, where she became friends with Sister Bernadine Casey. When Monica told Sister Bernadine that her dad hoped to become a Catholic priest, Sister Bernadine told her, "Have your dad pray that my deceased uncle, Father Solanus Casey, will intercede for him. He has a special love for men called to the priesthood who are faced with difficult circumstances."

"I'll tell my mom and dad about him."

"I know he'll ask God to bless your father. What is his name? I'll pray for him too."

"Peter."

When Monica told me about Father Solanus, I wanted to learn more about this man. I found that Barney grew up on a farm near Burkhardt, Wisconsin, the third of sixteen children.

As a child, Barney had suffered with black diphtheria, which left him with a weak, wispy, high-pitched voice and chronic sore throat. He also suffered severe migraine headaches most of his adult life. In spite of these obstacles, he was a natural leader, liked by everyone.

After crops failed and the family faced devastation, he quit school at 16 and left home to support the family. He first worked as a logger and later drove a streetcar in Superior, Wisconsin. Finally, at age 21, he was free to realize his dream of becoming a priest. He completed four years of high school at St. Francis De Sales Seminary, but after one year of college he was dismissed due to academic failure. Defeated and depressed, he returned to the family farm. How could he become a priest if he could not succeed academically, he wondered.

After a time, the Franciscan Capuchin Order accepted him, but he continued to fail in his studies. However, this time his superiors were impressed with his sensitivity and obvious holiness. Finally, he was ordained, but because of his perceived limited academic ability, the order denied him permission to hear confessions and give formal homilies.

His Capuchin superior puzzled over where to assign him. As a last resort, he assigned Father Solanus as doorkeeper, the most humble task in the monastery. Here he glorified God in a remarkable and unexpected manner. He soon became known as a holy man, a man who prayed ceaselessly and whose prayers were answered in dramatic ways. Soon people of all faiths and needs came to the monastery, especially the poor and homeless, seeking Father Solanus for counsel and prayer. During the Great Depression Father Solanus established a soup kitchen next door to the monastery in Detroit, which continues even now to serve the poor.

With a remarkable sense of humor, God took Father Solanus; a man seemingly not fit for the priesthood, a man whose faults and inadequacies marked him as a failure. He gave him the gift to comfort and heal, meeting the needs of the poor and needy in the most effective way possible. We cannot say, but perhaps his sanctity would not have developed had the Church not placed these unusual restrictions on his priesthood. The very limitations intended to prevent his influence on the laity were the catalyst for his remarkable ministry. He is believed to be the source of many healings and miracles of faith. Father Solanus has been named venerable and his case for sainthood is now in Rome.

One day, a friend and parishioner from Holy Family Cathedral called me. "I have two plane tickets to Detroit for my wife and my mother to attend a retreat at the Capuchin Monastery. My mother cannot go. I don't know why I'm calling you, but I thought you might like to go with Helen. Have you ever heard of Father Solanus Casey?"

"Oh my," I said. Chills ran down my spine. "Yes, and I would like very much to go."

The following weekend Helen and I left Tulsa for Detroit. We were able to spend an entire afternoon visiting Father Solanus' tomb, viewing his artifacts and talking with the Capuchin monks, one who had known him well.

Our friends, Helen and Marty, had given me an undeserved blessing, an opportunity to become even better acquainted with this humble monk whom I had come to know as my friend.

In many ways, our stories were similar: Peter's repeated attempts to be a Catholic priest; the impediment of having a wife and children. I found myself turning to Father Solanus in prayer for strength and the desire, not to know all the answers but to accept the situation, to know that God had called us to this place for His purpose and none other, and that the Holy Spirit would use us in spite of our imperfections and inadequacies. In my prayer book, I kept the tiny relic from Father Solanus' habit that Sister Bernadine had given us. There was no doubt in my mind that he prayed for us, sustaining us through many temptations and difficulties on our journey toward, and now in, Peter's priesthood. The weekend retreat, a gift from Marty and Helen, had brought to mind once again, the beauty and comfort of Father Solanus' life and ministry.

Then, just as things began to settle down in the parish after the religious education director had so dramatically left, Peter received a phone call from Bishop Beltran.

"Peter, what's this about the parish name being changed to Sacred Heart?"

"I don't understand, Bishop."

"The name of the church is St. William. You can't just decide to change it..."

"My predecessor told me that you gave him permission to change the name back to Sacred Heart."

"He did talk to me about it. However, I need a letter. You need to write to me explaining the rationale for the change."

"I thought that had been done. I'll do it right away, Bishop."

"In the meantime, go ahead and refer to the parish as Sacred Heart since the people think I've already given my permission."

"Thank you, Bishop. I appreciate that."

We had learned that in 1952, the present church building at Skiatook was made possible through funding from the Catholic Extension Society, USA, with one condition: that the church be renamed St. William after the bishop who headed the society at that time. To demonstrate how they felt about this, the people moved the life-size statue of the Sacred Heart of Jesus, which had stood near the old building, to its prominent place in front of the new St. William Church, where it remains today. Whether humor or stubbornness precipitated this is known only to those stouthearted parishioners who moved it, and the story is told and retold with delight and not a little Okie pride.

-21-

St. Jude Church

Tulsa, Oklahoma

While our adjustment in Skiatook was not without its challenges, the small congregation of St. Jude in north Tulsa was so thrilled to have a priest that Peter could do no wrong.

This area of the city was largely African American. Most of the white population who were financially able had moved out of the neighborhood in the sixties, at the height of racial tensions. The parish did not attract many Blacks, possibly because there were two predominately Black Catholic congregations a short distance away. Most of the folks who remained there in 1991 were poor, often widows, who would not, or could not, leave the neighborhood and the church they had attended most of their lives. Sadly, they were often barricaded in their homes, behind barred doors and windows for their safety.

When the people realized that Peter wanted to help them revitalize their small congregation, they cleaned, painted, and planted flowers on the grounds around their modest building. A group of retired folks met every Wednesday morning while the men performed maintenance and clean-up tasks. The women worked in the hall and kitchen, and then prepared lunch for the group. The day ended with the healing Mass that brought regular attendees from Holy Family Cathedral and others from across the city.

I remember that Rosalie Lupcho, communicant at St. Pius X, plugged in the electric organ that had been silent for years and played it for the healing Mass. She approached a shy American Indian woman, whom she learned had played the organ years earlier. "Marian, why don't you sit with me today? Maybe you would want to play again for Father Peter on Sundays."

"No, no. I couldn't do that," Marian Battese protested.

"I'll bet you could..." Rosalie gently nudged her. "Come sit with me anyway."

"I guess I could, if it's just to come and sit." Marian, a shy diminutive woman perched on the end of the organ bench and watched Rosalie throughout the service.

When the Mass ended, Marian said, "I couldn't play anyway. I shrunk so much in my old age I can't see over the heads of people. Either that or they're growing 'em taller these days."

The next week when Rosalie arrived for the healing Mass, she found the organ now rested on a twelve-inch riser and Marian was waiting to sit beside her. Soon Marian offered to play a familiar hymn, then some of the liturgical chants.

Before long, she faltered through some of the Sunday liturgy, but she never allowed Rosalie to give up the Wednesday healing Mass. Somehow, Rosalie's sharing in the music at St. Jude gave shy Marian the confidence she needed to return to playing the organ. Marian continued to play until shortly before her death.

These were the days before big Hispanic parishes in Tulsa and several Mexican families attended St. Jude, making the congregation a wonderful multicultural cross-section of people of all ages and ethnicities. The people were among the hardest working and praying folks we had ever served, finding little time for complaints or disagreements in the group. The Mexican families invited members of their community's mariachi band to participate in the Mass on the Feast of Our Lady of Guadalupe. They returned to entertain at the Mexican dinners the congregation initiated to raise money for the parish.

"Father Peter, you're not starting a Hispanic parish, are you?" Bishop Beltran asked.

Peter laughed and said, "No, we're just bringing St. Jude back to life. Deacon Jose and some of his friends have offered to help out once in awhile."

Another time, Peter held a special Mass for a Mexican woman who was anorexic and who believed that her disease was the result of a curse made by three Mexican witches when her mother was carrying her in her womb. As word traveled, the rumor started that Peter was performing exorcisms. "No, just the power of prayer," he replied.

It seemed that Peter's ministry was continually questioned by his brother priests, thus becoming the focus of gossip and mistrust.

Soon two attractive Black women came to see Peter. They wanted to start a Girl Scout troop but they did not have a place to meet. "We're good Baptists, Father, but in spite of that, do you think you might let us use St. Jude parish hall once a week?" The attractive young wife and mother smiled.

"We try to bring in the whole family, Father," the other woman said. "We believe that strong parental involvement now will keep families communicating when these children get to their teens."

"I think you've got a point there," Peter said. "Thank you for coming to me. This is a wonderful outreach for the parish and just the type of activity I want to support in North Tulsa. I will give you a key and you can come and go as you need to. Just be aware that St. Jude people have activities going on also and I would not want you to interfere with them. I'll give you the phone number of someone to call to coordinate your schedule."

"Father Peter, we are honored to be here with you," Brenda, the leader, said. "We believe we are teaching the future leaders of our community and we thank you for your support." Her friend nodded in agreement.

Peter found an outdoor manger scene in one of the storage closets at St. Jude Church, and as Advent approached, he prepared it to display in the yard.

"What are you doin' with that thing, Father?" Mary McGahey asked. "If you put that outside, they'll steal it or rip it apart. The kids in this here end of town swipe ever-thing in sight."

"Well, we'll try it," Peter said.

He cleaned up the figures and painted them, but with one change. He made the faces dark skinned. He found a wooden box for a manger and borrowed a spotlight. He then set up the scene in front of the church near the street. The scene generated a number of comments in the neighborhood about the Black Mary and Joseph. "What you s'pose that there Cath'lic preacher's up to?" St. Jude's people said their friends asked.

"We jus' laughed and told 'em we got a priest that cares about us now."

Peter stopped by Holy Family Cathedral one day and while he was having coffee with Olivia, the cook, she said, "My brother, Henry lives up there by St. Jude's, Father."

"Oh yes, I know Henry."

"He says that you have a manger scene with Black faces. Where you get that, Father?"

"Oh, I found them in a closet, and painted them with dark skin."

"Henry says one thing ain't right."

"What's that?"

"He says their noses ain't wide enough." Olivia laughed until tears came to her eyes. "Thas' good, Father. Our people, they needs that."

Neither the manger scene nor anything else at St. Jude Church was vandalized while Peter was the priest there. The *Tulsa World* reported frequent accounts of violence in North Tulsa: drive-by shootings, robberies, assaults. It went on day and night, week in and week out, but the church itself and our people were untouched by it. Few Black people attended St. Jude. Nevertheless, the pride of identity and support infused the neighborhood.

-22-

Sacred Heart Church

Skiatook, Oklahoma

The folks who had rented the small house on the corner of the property moved, and Peter and members of the congregation busied themselves to transform it into his office.

They faced the challenge of removing the mountain of things the renters had left behind, both inside the house and in the yard. The men brought pick-up trucks and a flat bed trailer, hauling four large loads of debris, including ruined carpets, to the dump.

However, the biggest challenge came in the form of a cockroach population. I had heard Oklahomans talk about the scourge of cockroaches, but I had no idea what a cockroach-infested building was really like. Even now, it makes my skin crawl to think about them. When we entered the building or turned on the lights at night, we would glimpse the creatures running for cover in the many cracks and crannies of the sad little building. They were everywhere. We could not get rid of them without the assistance of a professional. Such a man was Tom Florence, a retired exterminator, who attended Holy Family Cathedral. Peter called him and he arrived with his armaments and determination. Though Tom came back a second time, we were never entirely without cockroaches in Peter's office.

People in the parish came and painted all the rooms in the Little House, as it became known. One woman said she had done pretty well at the races recently and she bought mini-blinds for the windows with some of her winnings. We purchased carpet remnants and used one of our personal rugs to cover the floor in the priest's office.

When we were finished, and Peter had moved his desk and files in, we surveyed the results and decided that it would be all right for a temporary office. Something would eventually have to be done for a more adequate and professional environment for the priest.

In the midst of organizing our lives in Skiatook I received a telephone call from Rita Bisdorf, the friend who had edited my book. In the years since the book's publication, we had seen each other from time to time and talked often on the phone. Paul had died and Rita had continued living in their home with her son. Upon hearing her voice, I expected a lively chat with her.

"Mary, I wanted to let you know that I've decided to move to California," she said.

"Move?"

"Yes. My sister's husband is ill and she needs my help and moral support," Rita explained. "Well, actually, Ginger herself isn't well. I feel I must go."

"But, what will I—who will I—". I was too upset to utter a rational word. I could no more imagine life in Oklahoma without Rita than I could imagine life without Peter. Tears flowed as, between sobs I tried to tell her it would be all right. Still, I felt the pain of losing my mother all over again.

I thought of the comfort and strength she had been to me over the years. I had felt lonely and isolated when I met Rita, and she had welcomed me into her life. She loved the Catholic Church but she was not blind to the injustices that so often unfairly discouraged the people and then failed to meet their needs. We shared a common bond in our Irish ancestors, hers settling into Chicago politics, mine into ranching in the Willamette Valley of Oregon.

How will it be here without her? Her greatest gift was the support she gave me when I had to face difficult priests. What will I do without her, I wondered. I gathered myself together enough to ask, "When will you leave?"

"I have packed the things I'll be taking with me. Everything is being shipped and I'll fly out in a week."

"So soon?"

"Well, I've put off telling you." She hesitated. "I knew it would be hard."

"It's not fair to you for me to be so upset. I'm sorry that I don't have better control."

"Mary, call me whenever you need or want to talk, and I'll call you. We have a guest room in the apartment and I want you to come and visit."

"I'd like that very much."

"Come soon, Honey."

"Yes."

I was never able to fly out to visit Rita but we talked frequently on the phone. I missed her more than I had ever missed a friend before in my entire life. Her strength and counsel had sustained me through many difficult days.

After several years, she returned to Tulsa. She was ill and by now her son had married. Not wanting to be a burden, she moved into an assisted living facility. I saw Rita as often as I could. Her voice had grown huskier and her lovely white hair had thinned. She spent her days in her recliner, a stack of her most-loved books on the table beside her. When it became obvious that her health had deteriorated, she told me she had been diagnosed with cancer. "I've decided not to have chemotherapy. I'm tired and I'm ready to be with Paul again." Then she smiled and her eyes had that familiar twinkle. "My son Paul finally had the sense to marry Linda so I'm free to go."

Eventually she transferred to a nursing home and we went to see her there. Peter took Holy Communion to her and administered the sacrament of healing on each visit. The last time I saw Rita, she was quite low. Peter had left the room and I turned to go with him. Still, something drew me back to her bed side. I kissed her on the forehead and I said, "I love you, Rita. I'll pray for you."

Although she had not opened her eyes or responded to us during the entire visit, she said, "And I for you."

-23-

"They should have invited your wife."

"To a conference on celibacy?" Peter laughed, leaning back in his chair.

"No, I'm serious. Wouldn't Mary have something to say about celibacy?"

"Probably too much." Peter folded his arms across his chest and smiled. "You know the Irish! You're one too. And, she is no exception. God knew what he was doing when he gave her that red hair."

Peter had gone to the "Gift of Celibacy" conference in Tulsa reluctantly. He decided to go because he felt that it was a courtesy to his bishop to attend all of the priests' meetings and conferences if his schedule permitted.

The Irish priest seated next to him had entered seminary after twenty-five years of secular employment. Father Michael had chosen celibacy early in life.

On the other hand, maybe it had chosen him.

In any case, celibacy was his vocation and he lived it with dignity and balance. A simple priest with a ready smile, he served one of Oklahoma's poorest counties. Father Michael knew the people of his community and loved them, regardless of their faith or social status. Immaculate Conception Church in Poteau in southeast Oklahoma is an isolated rural parish that most priests endure for only a year or two. Now, in his seventh year, Father Michael conceded in an interview with the diocesan newspaper that life in a rural parish could be lonely. "It's a struggle, but I have many friends. I make community wherever I am."

A short, balding man, always cheerful and often seen with groups of kids in tow, we knew him as a lovable country priest, comfortable and confident in his own unique style of ministry.

At our dinner table in our home that warm spring evening, Peter told me about Father Michael. I listened and smiled with him.

"I like him. He is what he is," I said.

"He told me that when he gets up in the morning he prays all of the offices. He says his day gets busy and he sometimes can't work them all in, so he prays them in the morning, one right after the other." Peter chuckled.

"That's what I mean. I like him." I laughed, thinking of this man's dedication to the required discipline of prayer that is usually scheduled throughout the day. I thought of the many times I had served up a piping hot dinner only to have it get cold and lifeless waiting for Peter to finish praying his evening office.

"And he is friendly and gracious to me," Peter commented. "He always asks about you. I told him we'd have him come for dinner sometime when he comes to Tulsa on his day off."

"That's another thing I like about him: his independence."

Just then, the rectory telephone rang and Peter interrupted his meal to answer it.

I thought about Father Michael. I'd like to have him come to dinner. Like Peter, I craved the companionship of other priests and religious, those people with whom we could most share our life in the priesthood of the Catholic Church. However, although years had passed since Peter's ordination, I hesitated to issue another dinner invitation to a priest after Father Kirley would not come because he feared the other priests' criticism. I mentally scolded myself for what I acknowledged to be unreasonable reluctance. My life as the wife of a Catholic priest often brought more challenges my way than I wanted. Still, I thought, priest's wife is the life I am called to, and false modesty has never been my way. No matter where I am in God's greater scheme, I want to live and respond to the world around me in the most authentic way I can. Therefore, I'd take a chance when the time came. I'd invite Father Michael. He would accept my gesture of friendship. *(Author's note: Regrettably, the opportunity to invite Father Michael to our home never presented itself. I would have enjoyed it.)*

Peter had finished his telephone conversation and returned to his dinner, now cold, at the table. Absently, I looked past him out the window, to the rectory garden.

I had not expected to be the wife of a Roman Catholic priest. Nevertheless, it is what happened. I had not chosen nor wanted this life. I thought we would always be in the Episcopal Church's ministry. Still, it appears that like Father Michael's celibacy, God worked this miracle in me. I know now that if God wants something of me, He will take me there in spite of my most rational plans or my Irish temperament.

The wind moaned and the old Rectory quivered beneath its force. Large hailstones struck the flat kitchen roof over our heads. The teakettle on the stove began to whistle.

"Care for honey in your tea?" Peter asked, interrupting my thoughts.

"No thanks." I smiled at my husband across the table.

Now in this Oklahoma springtime, I wondered at the years. I felt as though I had been on a long journey, one that has sucked the marrow from my bones and then restored it with the life-giving waters of my faith. The journey that I began in the loss and grief of leaving the Episcopal Church had been transformed in this new ministry through grace and personal growth and renewal.

In our rectory garden, a red cardinal rested on the statue of St. Francis. The wind whipped the rain through our garage breezeway. With the reawakening and beauty of springtime we must also bear raging storms, thunder and lightning, high winds and tornadoes. A shiver ran down my spine, contradicting the spirit of this rare moment together. Somehow, this evening with its storm typifies our journey into the Catholic Church. Knowing contradiction, absurdity, fearsome beauty and sometimes, high drama, it is no surprise to me that the theme of the conference centered on what seemed to me to be rationalized statements and myths about both the celibate and married lifestyles. I heard the echo of Bishop Beltran's words repeated over the years: "You have no idea how unusual this is."

I'll concede that.

Still, how perfectly normal it feels to me to be a Catholic priest's wife. It is curious, that the vocation of priest's wife, not found in the Catholic Church, is present in spite of strong feelings in the hierarchy against it.

While I am told that the marriage ban for priests will never be lifted, I am certain that God has a purpose for my life here and now; that none of this is a whim of fate.

Yes, in spite everything, I am grateful for this journey into priesthood on which Peter dared to bring me.

And, on which I dared to come.

"Mary, do you want more tea?" It was Peter's voice, once again calling me back to this place and this moment in our rectory.

I could not help but think of celibacy in the Church's terms. The phrase, *"for the sake of the kingdom of heaven"* from the "Catechism of the Catholic Church". It continues: *"Called to consecrate themselves with undivided heart to the Lord and to the affairs of the Lord."*

How much better it is to have two undivided hearts consecrated to the Lord.

I am asked: What do you put first, Father Peter's priesthood or your marriage? I tell them that his priesthood and our marriage cannot be separated. Each is incomplete without the other. He is a better priest because we are called to his priesthood together. While I have not received the grace of sacramental ordination, one cannot deny that through our married state, I share in that grace in a unique gift as the Holy Spirit blesses our union and our shared vocation in a special way.

The rainstorm pelted the flat roof over the kitchen and I thought of the other morning when I followed Paul Guilfoyle out of the church after Mass. "This April's 'bout as wet and cold as it gits." He cupped his ear with one hand and leaned his lanky body forward, awaiting my response.

"Is that right?" I shouted. "Have you looked at the redbud tree lately?"

"Redbud? Well...uh, yes."

"Do you think it's going to live?"

"I don't rightly know, Mary, but I'll take another look at it."

In February, Paul had planted a redbud seedling outside the rectory kitchen. As it grew, it would reduce the glare of the late afternoon sun that streamed through the window over the kitchen sink.

"Redbud like the rain. Cold won't hurt it neither. Didn't see any blossoms, did you?"

I shook my head.

"I ain't seen no green on it yet, neither. Maybe the blossoms are slow." He pushed his maroon baseball cap back and scratched his forehead. "Shore did rain heavy last night. Lots a'cars on Osage this mornin.' I spect Twenty's closed cuz-a-high water. Better try Highway 'Leven this mornin', Mary." He touched his hat in the 'see ya later' gesture I had come to know. "Drive careful now..."

His short arthritic steps contradicted the strong, lean appearance of his body. I watched him hesitate at the curb before he stepped down to cross the street where his pick-up truck waited.

"Thanks, Paul!" I shouted after him.

He turned his stiff torso, cupped his ear, and nodded a 'welcome'.

I knew that 'lots a'cars on Osage' meant that the heavy rains of the previous night had flooded the banks of Bird Creek, making Highway 20 impassable. Even Highway 11 could have standing water. I would need to drive around the Skiatook Lake Dam and through the hills to my job in Tulsa.

"What are you thinking about, dear?" Peter's voice brought me back to the present.

"Oh, nothing, really. Just the rain—and Paul. I hope that redbud he planted gets come color soon. I was so afraid it wasn't going to live, but he says it will be okay."

In our first months in Skiatook, Paul had helped Peter prepare the raised flower and vegetable beds in the back yard. We drove with him in his shaky old Chevy pick-up truck some fifteen miles to his ranch, now managed by his daughter and son-in-law, to bring back rich soil and fertilizer from the cattle barns.

The long drive into the Osage hills, at a top speed of twenty miles an hour, turned out to be a journey back in time for me. Paul's old faded green Chevy pick-up was my dad's, reincarnated from the fifties. The play in the steering wheel was like driving an amusement park bumper car. I smiled watching him appear to steer from one side of the road to the other while guiding the truck in a straight path forward. It was Dad's old pick-up all over again.

Paul told us about growing up in these hills. All the time his window was open so the smoke from his Lucky Strike would drift into the air. He talked about the death of his young mother and growing up with his Osage Indian stepmother, about the farm, and milking cows before dawn, then driving the milk to the creamery in Tulsa, before he reached Holy Family School, where he and his sister Mildred finished all eight grades.

We saw wild turkeys along the way and a snapping turtle or two. He told us how the Indians value the turtle shell and use it in their dances. Paul turned off onto a rutted back road where he showed us an early oil well, still pumping oil out of the ground with the original system of belts and pulleys. It was unlike anything we had seen along the roads and highways of Oklahoma. I took photographs and hung them on the wall in my kitchen at the rectory.

When we arrived at the ranch, I amused myself by exploring the outbuildings and cattle pens while the men filled gunnysacks with soil mixed with rich manure, and then loaded them into Paul's pick-up.

Stepping into the hay barn, I entered another time and place. Three rusty bailing hooks hung on the wall, and in the corner lay a roll of discarded bailing wire. Under my feet, I felt the soft cushion of hay left there by years of stacking and loosening hay bales to feed herds of cattle without personal regard for the summer's heat or the winter's icy winds. The fragrant scent of hay, the shimmering dust that made shadowed designs as sunlight filtered through the wide cracks between the boards of the weathered old barn. It flashed through my memory: my dad's hands grasping the bailing hooks, my child's eyes watching him load the hay onto his flatbed truck, beads of sweat running down his face as he worked from first light until darkness. I saw again his hand-rolled cigarette hanging from the side of his mouth, still there when he filled the truck with gas. The gasoline scent filled my memory and I remembered my mother's alarmed concern for his careless disregard. These scents and images from my childhood came flooding back to me that day. It's the smells that transport the past forward that surprise and catch me when I least expect it. Here, so far away from the Oregon farm of my childhood, I found a part of myself I thought I had long ago set aside and forgotten.

That time with Paul was our first Fourth of July at Sacred Heart Church in Skiatook. Now, in our fourth spring here, in our backyard, we'd planted one of the raised beds with lettuce, spinach, and green onions, and the other with columbine, daisies and two new rose bushes, a birthday gift from my son, John, and his family in Seattle. Soon I would plant petunias and impatiens to fill in and add color to last through the long hot Oklahoma summer.

Redbud is Oklahoma's state tree. Folks here think of it as just another weed, but I love it. In the spring, around Easter, the purple blossoms of the redbud tree burst in profusion along the roads and streambeds and fringe the edges of irrigation ponds. After the dead, dry landscape of winter, its flowers seem to appear overnight. They last several days and in a morphogenosis become the green leaves that stay for the summer and into fall. An Oklahoma springtime is a resurrection, a reawakening of life after the winter's slumber. The redbud's purple blossoms are nearly always the first color to appear on the brown landscape.

It is Lent's liturgical color of preparation, followed by the Lord's own Resurrection at Easter.

The people—Father Michael and Paul— and the flowers of Oklahoma are the joys of my life in this extraordinary land. They make it home for me. They are the heart in "Heartland," especially so because Catholics are a minority in Oklahoma's small towns.

Skiatook's three large Southern Baptist churches and numerous other Protestant groups dominate the faith landscape here in the "buckle of the Bible belt." Roman Catholics are often misunderstood and sometimes persecuted for their beliefs, though persecution is rarer nowadays than in years past. I recalled one old-timer telling me that when he was a child, "Catholics and colored folks alike laid low so's not to give notice to the Klan." He was referring to the Ku Klux Klan, the secret brotherhood that had routinely terrorized Black, Jewish and Catholic southerners. I later learned that Catholics in small Oklahoma communities back then did not want their church bells rung because it called attention to their faith, and the bells just might lead to threats and even acts of violence. I admired these sturdy ranchers and farmers who courageously practiced their faith in spite of the pressures and prejudices of the overwhelming numbers of fundamentalist Christians in this small community.

I recalled one instance when Peter, the Catholic priest, was not allowed to sit with other Christian ministers at a community Thanksgiving service because it was offensive to some of them. When I asked him if he was going to attend, he smiled and said, "Oh yes. It keeps me humble."

However, Peter became close friends with Brother Jim, the minister at Emanuel Baptist Church in Skiatook. Brother Jim could be heard telling his people, "Father Peter is a Jesus man."

We visited their services from time to time and—with the bishop's permission—the two pastors exchanged pulpits one Sunday. While both Baptists and Catholics were uncomfortable with this, a good group came forward and attended from both congregations. Recalling the Sunday school I attended as a small child, Brother Jim told his people that I had been "saved" in the Baptist Church. Startled by this announcement, I managed to take it gracefully and smile warmly to the folks seated near me. It was true—the Baptist Sunday school was where my early faith life began.

Peter made friends with the young seminarian-minister at the Lakeview Baptist Church, as well. We had already come to respect David Wilson, a member there, who had served as our heating and air conditioning man for the church buildings. When our church acquired a new organ, Peter offered the old organ to the Lakeview congregation. It was an affirming gesture of good will for all Christians in our community. It was certainly an unheard-of generosity in small-town Oklahoma.

-24-

As Advent approached at Sacred Heart Church, Peter made plans and put them into action, introducing celebrations that became parish traditions.

The first one of the season occurred on December 6th when the Church celebrates the Feast of St. Nicholas, the fourth century Bishop of Myra in Asia Minor. Peter felt it was an important teaching to relate the jolly old elf our American children know as Santa Claus to the early bishop who loved and protected children and who gave generously to the poor.

When Peter began preparations for St. Nicholas day, he wondered how he might demonstrate the story of this lovable saint to the children in the parish. With his artistic talent and boundless energy, he fashioned stick puppets with papier-mâché heads and asked one of the Sisters of the Sorrowful Mother to sew authentic costumes for them. There were six characters needed for the puppet play: young Nicholas, a prisoner, a sailor, a young woman, a boy and a girl.

On the feast day when the Mass was finished, Peter surprised six children by inviting them to join him in front of the congregation. He introduced each character and told the story of Nicholas' good deeds, allowing each child the opportunity to share the dialogue in his or her own words. It was a delightful spontaneous enactment with everyone getting involved. However, I do not know what Bishop Beltran might have said when, at the end of the puppet play, Martha our organist struck the chords, and everyone joined in singing "Jolly Old St. Nicholas", as our own St. Nicholas walked down the aisle with gifts for the children. Even as I write, St. Nicholas' annual visit continues to be a loved tradition at Sacred Heart Church.

Christmas arrived and along with it, all the festivities and parties heralding that holiday. A group gathered in the church on the evening of the fourth Sunday in Advent to decorate for the Christmas midnight Mass. When the work was finished, we invited everyone to the rectory for refreshments and a late supper. Georgianna Ricketts, an Osage Indian woman handed Peter a gift. He opened the package to find a traditional wool Indian blanket.

"This is beautiful," Peter said to Georgianna. He stood and held the blanket, allowing it to unfold so that everyone could see.

"Not so fast, Father," Nadine Moyer said. "This is special."

Georgianna walked over to Peter and reverently placed the blanket around Peter's shoulders in the Osage Indian tradition. "We are honored that you are our priest," she said.

Peter, nearly speechless, said, "Thank you."

"We don't do this for just anyone," Georgianna said with a smile. Her eyes shone as she turned to her husband, Bud.

Christmas at Sacred Heart Catholic Church, Skiatook, Oklahoma

The children's Sunday school Christmas pageant was a wonderful chaotic mixed-up affair. One cannot analyze that which comes from children. They are completely guileless; it is only for us to love and appreciate their angelic faces when the scene is set and they sing "Away In A Manger...." Never mind that it is off key.

After a brief respite between Christmas and New Year's we began preparation for the Feast of the Epiphany, signifying the end of the twelve days of Christmas. Tradition tells us that three kings from different lands and cultures—a symbol that Jesus is for all people—traveled toward the east. They followed the star to Bethlehem where they offered gifts to the newborn Messiah.

Oklahoma has a large American Indian population and Sacred Heart is privileged to have a number of them in the congregation, many being full bloods. Peter asked Joe Berry, an Osage, Bill Wamego, a Pottawatomie, and Herman Henderson, a Cheyenne— all elders of their tribes—to wear their ceremonial dress to re-enact the coming of the three kings at our Epiphany celebration.

That Sunday, when the recessional hymn ended, all was quiet. Then, outside the church we heard the Native American bells jingling, signaling that something was about to happen. Ceremonial fragrance found its way into the church as the elders prepared the smoldering cedar to bless the people with smoke, using an eagle feather. Martha, our organist, played "We Three Kings" and the congregation sang. Children edged their way to the aisles and peered toward the entrance.

There they were.

Three kings.

Their kings.

Then the kings stopped before the crèche and paid homage to the infant Jesus, after which each elder greeted the children one by one, giving each a gift of gold, an orange.

I will never forget the children. Rion and Echo, grandchildren of Pottawatomie, Bill Wamego; Melyssa Hight, whose father is Osage and her mother Navajo and Pueblo, a tiny little girl with eyes as big and round as silver dollars. There were Alysha and Brandi Boese, whose father is Osage, and Evelyn Pitts with her granddaughters, Andrea and Erica, also Osage. Georgianna Ricketts was also there, misty eyed and beautiful. All of us, brothers and sisters in Christ, together, proud of the American Indian people in our midst, grateful for their heritage and the gifts they share with us by their presence in our parish and in our community.

-25-

In this lively parish setting, I no longer had time on my hands. As busy as my days had become with my full time job and Peter's parish ministry, my life had become normal in a way that I cherished and loved. Though still a mystery as to how it came into being, I was grateful for the soundproofed upstairs bedroom where I could slip away for a quick nap on a Sunday afternoon before my week at the university began.

I had always enjoyed every minute of parish ministry—well, almost every minute. More than anything, I felt that this was where God wanted me, with Peter making the church and our beautiful faith real to the people around us.

I enjoyed being with folks from all lifestyles, and I believe that this is one of the reasons I have been at peace in the Catholic Church. I had found my place at Sacred Heart and St. Jude. I felt at home among these people who accepted me without reservation and who had taken us into their hearts and nourished us from the first day.

Nor did they have preconceived notions of what a priest's wife does or who she is. Their hearts were open to whatever I chose my role to be among them. With our people at least, I did not need to wonder who I was in the Catholic Church.

Each summer Peter hosted a foreign missionary, usually a priest, or a nun who was home on leave and traveling through the diocese to raise money for their work. One such missionary was a priest from the Franciscan Missionaries of the Sacred Heart. He was openly curious about our life in this small rural parish. He asked me many questions. It amused me when he asked, "How do the women in the parish take you?"

"The women?"

"Yes. Do they resent you?"

"No... At least I don't think they do."

Actually, it had never entered my mind that the women might resent me. I certainly did not sense any resentment.

The priest continued. "I'm sure you've noticed how it is; Catholic women feel that the priest is their property. You know, to look after and take care of." He paused a moment and drank from his cup of coffee. He was a tall, balding man with a mild approachable way about him.

I laughed. "I'll be glad to let them have him."

He laughed with me.

"Seriously, Father, I haven't noticed any jealousy or resentment. However, anytime any of them want to do something for Peter, I encourage it. He's high maintenance and I can use all of the help I can get."

Father laughed. "It sounds like you've worked it out well."

"I see my life as a vocation. It only becomes a burden if I do not welcome all that it brings, and I have to admit, sometimes that is difficult. I'm pretty human."

"I believe the Church should give future priests the option to marry or remain celibate."

"I wish the Church was more open about the ninety or so married priests in the Pastoral Provision. It makes it hard to go places with my husband. To be introduced and get those knowing looks that say: sure, you're married. Girl friend is more like it."

We laughed.

"Or the time we went through customs in the Caribbean and the agent asked Peter, 'This your sister?' He said, 'No, she's my wife.' The agent's black eyes looked me over and he gave Peter a knowing nod. I could not help but think Peter should have let it go. Just let him think I was his 'sister'."

"It must be very difficult."

I laughed. "When you're as much of a prude as I am, it is. It would be so simple if the Church were more open. Why would a handful of married priests be a problem if the Church truly went public with who we are and why we have been allowed to remain married, a rare exception to required priestly celibacy?" He did not respond and I continued. "There's no question that it creates problems when the Pastoral Provision is clouded in near secrecy. If the hierarchy could bring themselves to open their hearts to the program and be more natural, it would be a blessing to the Church. Concealment always creates intrigue and suspicion.

Instead they don't want any publicity at all, saying that a married priest is scandalous to the laity, when in reality the real scandal is the Church's lack of openness."

"You certainly have a point there."

"I also think this secrecy is an insult to marriage and to women, particularly those of us who have sacrificed so that our husbands can be a part of the Pastoral Provision. It's not been easy for any of us."

"I never thought of it that way. You're right, Mary. It is an insult to the sacrament of marriage, to you who have sacrificed, and to lay people as well. The Church needs to have more faith in the laity."

As I talked with this priest, I recalled our visit to the Holy Land in 1986, less than a year after Peter was ordained. I was quite self-conscious about being married to a Catholic priest.

While traveling with Bishop Beltran and others from the diocese, we'd stayed at Our Lady of Notre Dame Hotel, which at that time, was owned and operated by the Vatican. I was embarrassed to be sharing a room with a priest, reasoning that the casual observer could not possibly know that we were married.

In a ridiculous need to avoid the appearance of scandal, I had found myself looking down the hall in both directions to make sure that no one saw me arriving or leaving with a man in a clerical collar. I also took care to keep my clothing out of sight so as not to shock the maids.

After one long day of sight seeing we'd arrived back at the hotel. I'd gone to our room to wash up before dinner and saw my damp panty hose hanging in the bathroom. Apparently I had accidentally left them lying somewhere and the maid had laundered them for me. So much for my illusion that the staff had not known the priest had a woman in the room. I realized then that you could not hide anything from the cleaning lady.

-26-

One of the great things about Sacred Heart Church in Skiatook was a group of women who called themselves the Stitch and Bitch Club, sometimes known as the Sisters of the Skillet for their renowned southern fried chicken. However, their official title was Sacred Heart Altar Society. The group was made up of older women who were wives of ranchers and other retirees, many of whom had lived in or near Skiatook all of their lives. They were women of modest means whose simple love of family and faith had bound them together in lifelong friendship. From time to time, they held other outings: overnights at Gertie's mountain cabin, dinner at a Chinese restaurant in Tulsa, whatever might strike their fancy. During our years there, I often heard women say, "I'm about to retire so I can go to the Altar Society." The companionship was clearly something to look forward to.

The Altar Society met every Wednesday to sew beautiful handmade quilts. They took a break at noon when one or two in the group would serve a hot meal. Of course, Peter had a standing invitation and frequently I would arrive home from work on Wednesdays to find my dinner waiting for me, a gift of their generosity and wonderful home-style cooking.

We had been told before we arrived in the parish that they sewed and gossiped, that they meddled and made life miserable for the priest, and that Peter should be wary of them. As with the other information we had heard about the congregation, we found the opposite to be true. They were good-hearted and generous, always ready for a lively discussion on politics or on horse racing versus casino gambling. Peter loved to get them started, then sit back, and listen.

Their income came mostly from the quilts they sewed for people in the community. It was a special honor to have a quilt made by the altar society and their list of those waiting for them filled several pages in a notebook they kept in their locked cabinet.

"That's a beautiful quilt you're making," Peter said to the group one day. "Whose is it?"

"This one? Oh, it's for a friend of ours."

Peter told me how much he liked this particular blue and beige quilt, and that one person, Betty Overton had pieced the entire cover by hand. He explained that this would make the quilt look uniform. When the whole group pieced the cover of a quilt, each person having a slightly different stitch, variations were sometimes evident in the finished quilt.

"I didn't think it would make that much difference," I said, feeling inadequate to any sort of sewing project. When I sewed the last Eucharistic vestment I made for Peter, I lined it with satin and appliquéd the orphreys by hand. I was not completely satisfied with the result. However, Peter treasured it all the same. Afterwards I gave my sewing machine to a young woman whom I rationalized needed it far more than I did, but in reality I simply did not like to sew.

That Christmas we opened a package to find the beige and blue heirloom quilt. The altar society had made it especially for us, all perfectly sewn by Betty Overton, quilted by the group, and finished by Little Rose Guilfoyle.

I've since read that a quilt is a treasury of memories and this one, sewn and given with love, certainly is.

One of my special memories of the altar society involves my late mother. When my sisters, Marie and Goldie, visited us with their husbands, Goldie told the Altar Society about a quilt that mother had started before she died, and said she would like to have it finished some day. The group interrupted their regular list of clients to sew the quilt for her, and Little Rose skillfully finished it off with a scalloped edge. Now, this other treasury of memories graces the home of Goldie's son Richard and his wife Chris through the talents and generous sharing of this group of faithful women.

However, quilting was not all these women did. They organized all the parish potlucks and prepared and served funeral dinners for every death in the congregation, whether the person was a member of the parish or not. Reva Polson's famous chicken and homemade noodles formed the basis for the menu.

They provided all the extras for the parish educational program, like Christmas candies and Easter treats. They prepared and served the annual St. Patrick's Day turkey dinner, never for a moment thinking that St. Patrick's Day and turkey dinner were an anomaly. The event was a major fundraiser for the parish, attended by the entire community and Catholics from neighboring parishes. Moreover, they were generous with their earnings, giving them to the support of whatever project Peter and the parish council asked of them.

Our seven years in Skiatook were some the happiest in our ministry. I'll never forget the people and their faith.

-27-

St. Joseph Church

Hominy, Oklahoma

When we had been at St. Jude Church for about two years, Bishop Beltran transferred Peter to St. Joseph Church in Hominy, twenty-six miles northwest of Skiatook. He would continue his ministry at Sacred Heart in Skiatook.

We had driven to Hominy once or twice on Peter's day off. With appealing historic buildings constructed mostly of grey Osage rock, many of which dated back to the earliest white settlers of the 1880s, it was a charming town. The first public school building, financed by private donations in 1904, remained in use nearly 100 years later as the community preschool building.

The streets, many with the original brick paving manufactured in Hominy, gave a bit of historical appeal to the town. There was also a festive and artistic ambiance with its Native American murals and gift and antique shops, most reflecting the Indian culture of the area. It was a nice small town where a priest or minister might retire, giving spiritual care to a small number of parishioners, and peacefully living out his days.

The Bishop's decision to assign Peter to Hominy was bittersweet for him. While Peter loved the people at St. Jude, he was excited about the possibilities that lay ahead for a ministry to the Osage Indians, the Oklahoma tribe catechized by the Church, beginning in the 1840s when the Jesuits served them in St. Paul, Kansas.

Again, there were warnings.

St. Joseph Church, reported to be a derelict and a priest killer, was said to be one we should avoid. We learned that in the recent past, one priest had loaded his belongings into his car, and then driven to the chancery in Tulsa, where he told the Bishop that he would leave the priesthood if he did not transfer him to another parish.

The congregation of St. Joseph was multi-ethnic. We soon learned that a group of white people controlled most things in the parish. It was not an easy beginning for Peter. Lay people were writing parish checks, while not depositing funds in a timely manner. There were bank overdrafts and few records of expenditures. In good conscience Peter could not allow haphazard management of parish funds. With the help of the bookkeeper in Skiatook, he initiated changes that some individuals felt he had no right to make. The situation was resolved with the help of the chancery, but it ended with deep-seated anger that continued throughout our ministry there.

The Osage are tall attractive people, proud of their heritage. Well before the white settlements, Frenchmen came into their villages to trade for the lush furs the Indians had trapped. Many of the French stayed, taking native women as their wives and leaving behind generations of strikingly handsome blue-eyed Osage people. We soon learned that Native Americans revere the tribal elders. They frequently responded to Peter's suggestions with, "We must first speak with the elders." Then after due consultation, his ideas would be put in force.

We had been there a short time when an occasion arose for Peter to ask one of the tribal leaders to perform a Cedar Ceremony, the traditional cleansing ritual by which the participant is smoked—blessed—using an eagle feather. A person might put his hands over the smoke, drawing it to him or herself in blessing.

The people welcomed Peter's desire to adapt customs and prayers that would be meaningful to both the whites and Indians. He trained the Osage boys to serve the altar and play on a soccer team he initiated with the Methodist minister.

He organized groups within the parish to further the Osage customs and culture, naming them Kateri Circles, dedicated to Blessed Kateri Tekakwitha, the young Mohawk girl who died of smallpox in 1680. Smallpox had horribly scarred the young maiden. However, after her death, as her body awaited burial, her skin miraculously became clear and unblemished.

One of the people in the parish gave Peter a life-size statue. He refurbished and painted it to depict Blessed Kateri, using the colors from the blanket that Georgianna Ricketts had given him and placing it in the entrance to the church.

Lottie Pratt, one of the elders, taught an Osage language class at the church and helped Peter learn to pray the Lord's Prayer in Osage as a gesture of respect and love for their native culture.

With Peter's assignment to St. Joseph Church his ministry became busier and I often went with him just to talk and to drive for him when he visited the parish.

In the fall of 1993, the Vatican appointed Bishop Beltran Archbishop of Oklahoma City. Our diocese awaited the appointment of a new bishop. This was one of my greatest fears. Bishop Beltran had assured us that because Peter had been incardinated into the diocese, any future bishop would be required to recognize Peter as a priest of the diocese, even though he might not support the Pastoral Provision. After the archbishop of Seattle had turned us down and the now retiring archbishop of Oklahoma City had forbidden Peter to speak in the archdiocese, I was concerned about what the future might hold for us under a new bishop. While he probably would not openly do harm to the ministries of the married priests, we had been in this situation long enough to know that a bishop could find a way to do anything he might wish.

Within a short time, a new man was appointed Bishop of the Diocese of Tulsa. Shortly after he arrived in January 1994, he met at St. Joseph Church with the priests who served congregations in Osage County. It snowed the night before and the Tulsa priest assigned to drive him to Hominy cancelled. It then became Peter's responsibility to drive to Tulsa to get him and return him to Tulsa after the meeting, a total of more than eighty miles in unpredictable weather.

In Hominy, Herman DeRoin and his wife Claudia cared for Viola DeRoin, Herman's mother who was bedridden with complications due to diabetes. Like so many Indians with diabetes, Viola, in her eighties, had lost both legs to the disease. Peter learned that the day of the meeting was Viola's birthday, so he suggested to Claudia that he would try to bring the bishop to her home for a special birthday blessing.

"Have Mrs. DeRoin ready for a visitor, but don't tell her who's coming because I'm not sure he will have time, and I don't want to disappoint her. Bishop Beltran loved doing these special things for people but I don't know how this new bishop feels about it."

"Yes, I understand. I won't tell her who's coming, but we'll be ready. This is so exciting. Our new bishop is coming to my house." She clasped her hands to her chest and looked heavenward, anticipating how special this would be to her mother-in-law.

The day of the meeting, Peter told the bishop about Mrs. DeRoin. "Today is Viola's birthday and Claudia's house is on our way. You will also be able to see the Indian cemetery, the ceremonial grounds, and the Indian roundhouse. Claudia's house is adjacent to the Indian land."

Minutes later Peter stopped the car at the DeRoin house. The bishop turned to Peter. "I would like you to administer the sacrament of healing to the old lady," he said.

In the house, Peter's nerves got the better of him. Flustered, he did not pray the prayer as prescribed by Catholic ritual. It was an adequate prayer, but not the exact words.

Mrs. DeRoin and Claudia were thrilled by the visit. "I am so happy." The old woman clasped her hands with joy. "Now I will have a story to tell."

Returning to the car, the bishop reprimanded Peter because he did not use the exact wording for the prayer. Peter knew that other priests frequently used other forms of prayer, and often anointed simply in the name of the Holy Trinity, but he said nothing. The bishop required Peter to meet with another priest for instruction on all seven sacraments, a demeaning task for a man who had taught these sacraments throughout his ministry. As always, Peter realized that his bishop knew nothing of his past ministry and did not ask. He yielded to the discipline without complaint.

After two meetings, the priest instructor told Peter that he did not think it was necessary to meet again. I am sure that he knew Peter was as capable as any other priest in administering the sacraments.

Later, Peter was having lunch with the head chaplain at St. Francis Hospital. When Peter told him what had occurred, he said, "Why I use a number of different prayers. I try to select a prayer that is appropriate to each situation. I'm appalled that our bishop did that to you."

A short time after the incident with Viola DeRoin, a priest whose job was assistant to the bishop, appeared at the rectory in Skiatook unannounced. "I've come by to see how things are going, Peter."

"Oh, I guess as well as can as can be expected. Mary and I like it here very much. Is this an official visit?"

"Uhh, well yes. It is."

"Okay."

"We've had it reported that you are not using grape wine for the Eucharist. Are you aware that the wine must be made from grapes?"

"Yes." Peter hesitated. "But wait here. I'll be right back."

Peter went to the sacristy in the church and returned within a few minutes. He handed the priest the bottle of wine. The label indicated that the grapes had been grown and the wine made by Benedictine monks in Arkansas. "Is that Catholic enough for you, Father?"

"Oh. I guess we have been misinformed."

"Yes, well, you could have called me and I would have been glad to bring a bottle by your office." Peter smiled.

In these small incidents where charity and peace were absent, our time with our new bishop became increasingly difficult. In this and in the pastoral care of an old Indian woman, it was sad that her joy should be diminished through ecclesiastical suspicion and insensitivity.

-28-

St. Joseph Church and the town of Hominy, an Indian word believed to mean night stalker, are located in the heart of the Osage Nation. Twenty-six miles northeast of Skiatook, Hominy is the southern point of a triangle formed by three important historic Native American sites for the Osage. The northwest point of the triangle is Grayhorse, near the town of Fairfax; the third point, Pawhuska, is almost directly north of Hominy and is the capitol of the Osage Nation. The ceremonial grounds, roundhouse, and tribal cemetery are located in Hominy.

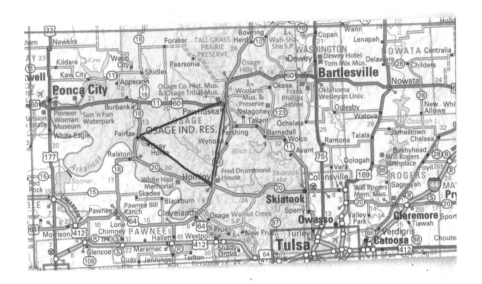

Osage Triangle

During our first summer at St. Joseph we were introduced to the I-Lon-Shka ceremonies held annually by the Osage Nation. When the elders invited us to attend, we considered it a special honor.

A tradition given to the Osage people by the Ponca and Kaw tribes, the I-Lon-Shka has been their principal tribal ritual for over a century. Unlike the more recent powwow, a festive social dance, the I-Lon-Shka is a solemn religious ceremony. The word, I-Lon-Shka, translates "playground of the eldest son." However, the atmosphere is reverent and respectful.

The ceremony's most important feature is the drum, so in each district a young man, ideally an eldest son, is chosen to be the drum-keeper. The drum-keeper and his family care for and protect the drum, provide food for the ceremony, and oversee the dances.

The I-Lon-Shka takes place in an open pavilion called an arbor. Families from throughout the United States gather to camp on the ceremonial grounds near the arbor for the four days of ceremonies. On the last day, special songs belonging to particular families or individuals are sung, and gifts are given from family to family in potlatch tradition.

The I-Lon-Shka dance costume is Osage traditional tribal dress. Often quite elaborate and costly, these costumes are passed down from generation to generation, becoming an important tradition in the family and tribe.

Men wear colorful broadcloth leggings, breechcloths and tailpieces, and leather moccasins. Their shirts are decorated simply but beautifully with ribbons. The hand-beaded belts, shell necklaces, silver armbands, and silk scarves add artistic as well as historical clarity to each ceremonial costume. A long narrow otter hide hangs from the back of the neck to the floor. Each male headdress is a roach of porcupine quills and a single eagle feather mounted on an elk horn spreader. Both men and women carry eagle-tail fans. When a boy has completed the ceremony, he they say that he is "roached."

Although the I-Lon-Shka is traditionally a dance for men and boys, in recent years women and girls have participated. Their clothing is the traditional tribal dress of bright colored broadcloth skirts trimmed with fancy ribbon work and hip-length shirts. Each wears an ornate hand-beaded necklace tied in back with two long satin ribbons. The long shirt hides an exquisite Osage finger-woven belt of which only the beaded tails show in back, reaching to the hems of the skirts. They also wear soft leather moccasins and silk shawls of many different colors whose long fringes sway in rhythm with the dance. At a signal, the girls and women move from the sidelines into the outer edge of the circle and begin to slowly dance around the ring.

The I-Lon-Shka represents tribal loyalty and is an important spiritual and cultural reinforcement for the Osage people today. Here, standards of conduct and ways of living are set. The four days are marked with reserved suitable behavior, as well as reverence for the drum, for life and for Osage tradition. Alcoholic beverages, photographs, and video photography are not allowed inside the pavilion.

When we arrived at the ceremonial grounds that evening, Lottie Pratt and her family greeted us and showed us the way to their table where a meal of corn soup and fry bread would be served. In Oklahoma, we speak of "Indian time" which means "it will begin when everyone is here and we are ready." The family had waited for us before they began the speeches that are an important part of all traditional Indian gatherings where food is served. The talks are offered in an atmosphere of leisurely honor and pride of family and friendship. It is customary to invite the priest to speak, and Stephen Pratt, Lottie's son, did just that. However, after all the speeches, the food was getting cold and Peter, ever mindful of his stomach, spoke briefly and completed his thoughts with the blessing of the food.

"Why did you speak for such a short time, Father?" Stephen asked.

"I was afraid the food was getting cold."

Stephen smiled and replied, "It is the talk that is important."

As the sun slid behind the Osage hills, we moved to the bleachers to watch the dances. Nearly two hundred Indian men and boys in full Osage regalia entered the arena, walking not in solemn procession but with immense dignity. They sat on benches around the edge of the dance area, facing toward the center and the drum, their backs to the dancers. Because women are not permitted to sit with the men, every seat on the square perimeter was occupied by a man.

As I looked around the pavilion, awestruck by the scene before me, I could not speak. It seemed almost a sacrilege to witness this solemn scene. It was as though we had opened a locked door and stepped into another time and place. Peter took my hand and squeezed it and I knew he felt the same.

In the center of the dance ground, the singers sat in a circle around the drum, their backs to the dancers. The signal was given, the drum pounded and the singers' wail joined in.

The scene was impressive, at once holy, and somehow a bit disquieting. Then the jingling of the dancers' bells intensified. The braves began the dance, moving around the pavilion, the drummers and singers still in the center. Their movements melded with the ghosts of their ancestors in both solemn and lighthearted rhythms, bringing together fathers and grandfathers, great-grandfathers and these sons, the seen and the unseen in this contemporary Osage community. I felt a part of all the history on this continent in that moment and I was proud of my Native American brothers and sisters and their desire to preserve their traditions.

In the past, some priests had been critical of the Indians' involvement in the Native American Church while at the same time, claiming to be practicing Catholic Christians. However, Peter felt charitable toward this dual nature of religious practice. He did not teach against their native religious customs. Instead, he encouraged them in their Christian faith life and demonstrated ways in which they could incorporate their native traditions into their Catholic spirituality. He felt that keeping them active in the parish was the most important thing he could do for them. Simply, he did not judge or attempt to reform their native ways, but rather to build on their Catholic faith in a positive way.

-29-

After a trip to Alaska to be with our daughters on Thanksgiving in 1996, we decided to purchase the Tulsa home of friends whom we had visited in Anchorage. Although Peter would not retire until 1998, we reasoned that we could work on the house at our leisure and prepare it for the time when we would need it, a year and a half in the future.

We hired Roger Wiley to remodel the kitchen and bathroom. He removed a back bedroom window, turning it into a door and built a spacious deck overlooking the shady backyard with its seventy-five year old sweet gum trees. The electrical wiring was frighteningly outdated necessitating complete rewiring. We scraped, cleaned, and painted until our hands were raw and our knees screamed for relief.

It was a sturdy arts and crafts style home built in 1923, with the spacious rooms and small clothes closets of that period. Few houses in Tulsa had basements, but this house had a wonderful basement. It would become our fraidy hole—our refuge should a tornado threaten—no more dark holes full of snakes. We worked on the house in our spare time, not thinking we would need it any time soon.

However, the following spring, 1997, in holy week, Peter became ill with facial and body rash, and swelling. We thought the condition was a bad case of poison ivy caused when he had been exposed to smoke from a brush fire near Lake Skiatook earlier in the week. He barely made it through the Holy Thursday and Good Friday services. On Saturday morning, he asked me to call Father Joe Howell, hoping that he could take the Easter Sunday Masses for him. As unlikely as it was in this busy season, Father Joe was free and agreed to come to Skiatook and Hominy for Peter. He smiled and shook his head when he told us that it was the first Easter Sunday he had been free in his forty-some years in the priesthood. "Somebody's looking out for you," he said.

By Sunday morning, Peter's condition had worsened and we asked our friend and parishioner, Dr. Rudy Wolf, to come by the rectory on his way to Mass. Rudy suggested that I take Peter to the emergency room at St. John Medical Center and call his personal physician, Dr. David Browning.

Peter was admitted to St. John Medical Center, and by Monday morning, his condition had further deteriorated. While there had been a parade of medical specialists in and out of his room, none could identify his condition, only that it was not poison ivy. Dr. Browning ran a series of diagnostic tests, all with negative outcomes. Finally, a dermatologist, Dr. David Minor, determined that Peter's condition was an autoimmune response to an anti-inflammatory medication he had taken for joint pain. By discontinuing the medication, he began to get better and by Thursday, I was able to take him home. Why his body reacted to the medication remained a mystery, and Dr. Browning continued diagnostic testing, the final being a bone marrow biopsy.

The morning we went to Dr. Browning's office for consultation, we had convinced ourselves that it would not be serious and that the medical treatment would be simple. After all, it was only an allergic reaction. Moreover, we knew what had caused it. Or, so it seemed.

Seated in the doctor's office, confident that a solution was imminent, we waited.

Dr. Browning came into the exam room and sat down. "Father, I'm very sorry to have to tell you that you have myeloma and it is not a curable disease." Dr. Browning's voice filled with emotion. "Cancer of the bone marrow is one of the cancers we can not cure as yet. The average survival is six months to two years."

Moments passed and Peter asked, "What is the treatment?"

"There are several things we can do," Dr. Browning said, "but first, I want you to go to the cancer clinic at St. Francis Hospital. Their program is as fine as any in the country and I think they will steer us in the right direction."

We waited for him to go on.

"Are you having symptoms? Back pain? Bone pain anywhere? Weakness?" Dr. Browning asked.

"No pain. The only thing I can say is that lately I become unusually exhausted after a short time. I'm ready for a nap after the daily Mass. I get up at 4:30 and by 8:30 I'm bushed. I only nap for twenty minutes or so. But then, after lunch I'm ready for another one." Peter laughed.

"I've noticed that he says he's tired more frequently," I said, "I just assumed it was a matter of growing older. But this...."

"I'm not having any pain, though. I can't think of anything else that might be a symptom."

"When can we get an appointment at to the cancer clinic?" I asked.

"I'll have Dottie make an appointment for you right now."

Dr. Browning left the room and I turned to Peter. "Are you *sure* you're not having pain?"

"Yes. I would tell you if I were. This is crazy. What a shock. I just thought the tiredness was normal." Peter turned to me and smiled.

"I know..."

We hardly knew what to say or what questions to ask. It all seemed unreal to us.

After our meeting, I did not go back to work that day. Peter felt it was his obligation to inform the bishop of his illness as quickly as possible, and wanted to ask for his counsel and prayers. He asked me to go with him.

The meeting with our bishop was not a satisfactory one in my mind. Bishop talked about death and Peter's last Mass, how he would feel at that time. He did not ask about cancer treatment, or if he needed assistance in the parishes. It was a strange meeting and I could not help but wonder if meeting with him had been a wise decision. A few days later, Peter asked Dr. Browning to write a letter to the bishop explaining that while his activities might be curtailed from time to time, it was desirable for Peter to continue in his ministry.

The next morning I went into work late so I could attend the morning Mass, this first Mass since we had learned he had terminal cancer. We could not hide our emotions as we shared our grief with other daily communicants. We all cried. My mind wandered as my thoughts repeated:

It can't end like this.

God wouldn't do this.

I know He wouldn't.

We spent the weekend crying and holding each other. We called the children. We tried to reassure them, but in the end, it was pointless. Something that felt foreign and evil had invaded our lives. In a state of shock I wandered through the rectory, unable to focus, or to find meaning and purpose in the tasks that needed my attention.

So sudden, I thought. Life moves along and then "whump" —it hits. So little time together, it seemed. There would be no retirement years to play in. We had had forty years of marriage in a busy and demanding ministry. Unrelentingly so. With few moments of peace and relaxation. I thought of the weeks at the cabin on the Sixes River Ranch in Oregon.

They will have to be enough.

Enough for all time.

I thought of the words I had turned to over the years when we had faced crises. Their truth had encouraged and sustained me when Peter decided to leave the Episcopal Church. On the front page of the Seattle Catholic newspaper, *The Progress*, I had seen a photograph in which a work-worn hand cradled a sprouting seed. The caption read:

"People look ahead to the future with hope and expectation.
They plan for the future and hope to shape it. But like the seed
that grows, the future is surprising, always a bit different,
sometimes a lot better than we expect."

Nothing about my life turns out the way I plan, I thought. Here I am again, God, and I have to fit into your plan. Don't I ever have anything to say? Better than we expect? No. It's not better. I wanted to shake my fist at God. Shout: No! Not now!

Still, there was something about these words that gave me strength and a certain hope.

Word spread rapidly around the town and among our friends throughout the diocese. Everyone promised prayer and we took solace in that. People from Emanuel Baptist Church came, laid hands on Peter, and prayed with him. Like others, we learned through tragedy, that we had many friends among our Baptist and other Protestant neighbors in Skiatook.

Our friends and parishioners, Dr. Rudy and Mavis Wolf, returned from Rome where they had visited Father Peter Wells, a young priest from Tulsa. Father Wells was then a student at the Pontifical College. The men in this program would be appointed to papal embassies around the world and would likely become the future cardinals of the Church. Mavis and Rudy had told Father Wells that Peter had been diagnosed with myeloma.

That week Father Wells celebrated Mass for Peter at the tomb of Pope John XXIII with Mavis and Rudy beside him. Later that day he met with Pope John Paul II for his regular private audience, a requirement for the students at the college. Father Wells told the Holy Father about Peter's illness, explaining that Peter was one of the Pastoral Provision priests in the Diocese of Tulsa, and asked that he pray for him. He reported that the Holy Father said, "Yes. I know about the Pastoral Provision." When he finished speaking with the pontiff, Father Wells returned to his seat in the auditorium and other students commenced their papal visits.

A short time later, the Pope's assistant, a priest, came to Father Wells. "What is the name of the priest who has myeloma?" he asked. When Father Wells told him, he wrote Peter's name in the Pope's black intercession book. "The Holy Father will pray for Father Peter," he said.

It is difficult to describe my feelings when Dr. Wolf delivered Father Wells' message telling us of John Paul II's intercessory prayers. The Holy Father would pray by name for one priest out of thousands, perhaps millions? How ironic that Peter should have suffered at the hands of our own bishop, yet be honored in this way by the most powerful prelate in the Catholic Church. Goose bumps literally skittered up and down my spine. How is it that we deserve this blessing, I wondered. Anything might happen because of this holy man's prayers.

Dr. Wolf told us that Father Wells took him and Mavis to Castillo Santa Maria on Ascension Thursday, where he again celebrated a Mass for Peter's healing. This ancient chapel had been the site of the Apostolic Nuncio, where young priests, including popes, men who would become the extension of the Holy Father throughout the world, had prayed. Dr. Wolf said, "We were on the exact spot of Holy men who have led the Church, praying for Father Peter on the day we celebrate Christ's conclusion of the mission of our salvation by His ascension into heaven. We shall never forget it."

I thought of our pilgrimage to Rome in 1984. Bishop Beltran had arranged an audience with Pope John Paul II. For many of our fellow travelers, the papal audience was a life-long dream come true, and certainly the highlight of the entire pilgrimage. For myself, I wondered how exciting it could be to be one of five thousand pilgrims in St. Peter's Square. The Pope was only a human person. How could this mob-event capture the mystique of the Papacy?

The day of the Papal audience arrived, raining. We purchased an umbrella from a street vendor on the way and prepared to wait in the rain for hours amid thousands of pilgrims, hoping for a glimpse of John Paul II.

We arrived at St. Peter's Square and found our seats that were amazingly close to where the Holy Father would pass. During the several hours' wait, Polish Catholics seated near the podium waved colorful flags and sang Polish songs—national songs, as well as hymns. Groups from other nations sang as well. Banners and flags waved everywhere around us. Expectation filled the air with a kind of fervent white magic. Many people wore the festive ethnic dress of their countries. As excitement filled the air and built all around me, I was caught up in the anticipation of the drama waiting to unfold. The Swiss Guard appeared and we knew that it must be nearly time for the Holy Father to appear.

We understood that the Pope-mobile would proceed down the aisles cordoned off for that purpose.

Then he came. Pope John Paul II. He passed a few inches beyond our reach. He gave us his Papal blessing, reaching out, and touching those pilgrims who were near him. Many around us stood on chairs. Others fell to their knees. Almost everyone waved religious articles for the Holy Father to bless. As he moved on, I heard a nun in front of me who was able to touch him, say, "I'm never going to wash my hand again."

Since that day, I no longer scoff at a five thousand-person audience with the Holy Father. I had not expected this dramatic experience, his charisma and the mystique of the Papacy, signifying the power of God in our lives. I had to admit that the man possessed a palpable aura of sanctity.

So now in 1997, as my husband faced the unknown effects of incurable cancer—I could not yet bring myself to say terminal—I knew in my heart that the Holy Father's prayers and the prayers of our family and friends would bring us dramatically closer to God's will for our lives than we had ever been at any other time. I did not have great expectations of physical healing. I knew only that this tragic turn of events for Peter and for me would bring many blessings and that Pope John Paul II's prayers were only the beginning.

Two weeks after the doctor had first diagnosed Peter's myeloma, two weeks that seemed to go on forever and only a few days after we learned of the Holy Father's prayers for Peter, we met with the oncologist. After further testing, he recommended that the myeloma not be treated.

"It could be what we call "smoldering myeloma" but we won't know that for a few months. We'll monitor it and see where it goes," the doctor said.

Can this be the result of the Holy Father's prayers, we wondered.

But, not be treated? This did not seem right to me. Don't we all know that when cancer is caught in the early stages there is better chance for survival? That's the point—catch it early I thought. I could not believe that my husband's cancer should not be treated.

"Shall I come back here to be monitored or is it possible that Dr. Browning can do that?" I heard Peter ask.

"I don't see why Browning can't monitor you. If it progresses, he'll send you back here," the doctor said. "In the meantime, it is very important that you take precautions not to break any bones. That could cause the myeloma to flare up. Do not have any type of surgery if you can avoid it. In addition, stay away from the flu. Your immune system is in the low normal range at this time but since you were so dramatically affected by the anti-inflammatory drug, your body could react to almost anything and you could have another episode."

He declined to predict how long Peter could go without treatment. "Sometimes it's slow. At very best, six to ten years. Tumors will form in the bone marrow and penetrate the bones, then spread throughout the body. You need to do everything you can to keep your bones strong. Six hundred milligrams of calcium with vitamin D twice a day is important. We just have to wait and see what happens."

We left the doctor's office, feeling unsure whether we should be happy or further saddened. I wanted to get another opinion but Peter said no, he would take this doctor's diagnosis and advice.

I was not satisfied, however. I searched the internet and requested information from the National Myeloma Foundation. What I learned was this: Older myeloma patients do better if chemotherapy, radiation and other treatments are postponed until certain blood protein levels indicate further progression of the disease. Younger patients, people in their forties and fifties, sometimes do well with a complicated procedure called a autologous stem cell transplant. Since there is no cure and the treatment destroys good cells as well as cancerous ones, the older patient, in contrast to the younger, tends to remain healthy longer and maintain a better quality of life without treatment.

Still, with all the implications that the word "cancer" brings to mind, it was difficult to believe that treating this disease could actually shorten Peter's life.

Gradually we became accustomed to this way of doing things and as Dr. Browning monitored Peter, carefully observing the changes in his bones and blood chemistry, we gained confidence that it was the right thing to do.

However, having the knowledge that no treatment is the right treatment and actually accepting it were two different things. Peter insisted that his old careless ways were in the past, that he had changed and would take appropriate personal safety precautions. However, when the gutters on the education build-ing needed painting, he climbed a ladder and, lying on the edge of the roof, leaned out to do the job. Dr. Wolf happened to drive down the street and spotted him. He stopped his car and jumped out, waved his arms at Peter and shouted, "Father, get down from there right now!"

"Okay, okay. I'm coming," Peter shouted in return.

"The trouble with the new Father Peter is that he's just like the old one." Rudy waited until Peter climbed down, and then made him promise to leave the gutters to someone else.

Simply put, short of a strait jacket, it was impossible to con-trol Peter's activities.

-30-

In the weeks following the diagnosis, I realized that what had seemed premature timing in the purchase of a house was not in the least untimely. It could provide a place for Peter to rest on his day off, away from the telephone and the doorbell in the rectory. We moved some of our personal furniture into the Tulsa house. We often went there on Sunday after Mass and spent the night. For Peter it was a healing respite from the pressures of the parish.

By late summer, Peter had decided that he needed to reduce his workload. He asked the bishop to replace him at St. Joseph Church in Hominy, while allowing him to continue in Skiatook.

Leaving the people in Hominy was a gut-wrenching experience for Peter. He could not help but wonder if the Indians would be understood and cared for, but he simply did not have the energy for two parishes.

I went with Peter to St. Joseph Church on his last Sunday there. I sat quietly in the congregation as families and individuals arrived for Mass. Old and young, each face, each set of bent shoulders, brought to mind memories of the several years we had spent with them.

An elder, Lucille Robideaux, who when Peter was distressed about white families leaving to go to another parish, had comforted him with, "Don't worry, Father. We were here when they came. We'll be here long after they come back and then go away again."

I thought of the frantic phone call in the middle of the night when a drunken Osage Indian woke us to say that he had just stabbed his wife and killed her. Actually, she was not dead. He had cut her badly and then lost consciousness. When he awoke and she was not there, he thought he had killed her. The ambulance had already taken her to the hospital. Several days later, Peter visited the man in the Pawhuska jail and found him held under shocking conditions. Dressed only in his underwear, he sat in a dirty cell with a bare cot and rudimentary toilet facilities. This was but one episode of the tragedy and sadness that alcohol and drugs caused in a number of Indian families, and one that Peter felt strongly could be remedied only through their own cultural heritage and spirituality in tandem with our Catholic faith.

I remembered the First Holy Communion class of one small Indian boy; it was the first year after the disgruntled families left. How his teacher, Audrey Johnson told him with quiet joy, "We're so happy for you. You are very special to us." Audrey, a Navajo and Pueblo Indian lived in Skiatook and helped Peter prepare the children for Holy Communion and first Confession. The following year Audrey taught a class of five small Indian boys for First Holy Communion. When they posed with their teacher for a photograph, the pride I saw in their faces touched me deeply.

After the Mass I went to the hall for the coffee hour. I looked, for the last time, at the mural of Osage Indian history that Peter had painted on one wall there. In bright reds, yellows, blues and soft earth tones, the painting told the story of how the Jesuit priests had established the mission to the Osage tribe in St. Paul, Kansas prior to 1847. The painting depicts how the Ulysses S. Grant administration moved the tribe to Oklahoma Territory in 1872, where the villages at Fairfax near Grayhorse, Hominy, and Pawhuska were established to form the Osage triangle so important to their continuing cultural survival. Ignoring that the Jesuits had catechized the Osage, President Grant assigned a Quaker minister to them and stated that they would now be Quakers. No Catholic priests came with them to Oklahoma. In spite of this, they remained Catholic. A priest was assigned to the Osage people fifteen years later in 1887. It is well to note that in spite of years of pressure and neglect, the Indians established Catholic parishes and built beautiful churches in all three communities.

I warmed my hands on the coffee cup and smiled at the simple figures in Peter's painting. I believe the art world would kindly label it a primitive. Still Peter's paintings of this sort had an undeniable charm. As I thought about his need to portray the rich history of these people, I wondered if the families that had left the parish would now return to take over the leadership roles. The Indians had seemed to gain so much pride and satisfaction from assuming leadership. I wondered if the mural would remain. It was sad to leave them seemingly defenseless, yet their survival and the fact that they were taking on these roles indicated their ability and desire for self-determination. So often, it seemed that Native Americans were swept along by history, both national and local, each having a driving force in their lives. Yes, in all of our lives.

Native American men seated at a table in the parish hall at St. Joseph Church. Behind them is the mural of the beginning of ministry to the Osage people by Father Peter.

Father Peter greeting people after Mass. Above the door is the mural of the Holy Family that he painted.

As we got into our car to drive away, Claudia DeRoin stopped us. She reached through the open window and placed her hand on Peter's arm. In her soft, native, voice she said, "Father, you were one of the priests who loved us. We will never forget you."

For Peter, no treasure could have been more precious than Claudia's words. Yes, he had loved them. Not in perfection, but with a deep appreciation for their culture and the heritage they shared with us through their stories and their lives, interwoven across the centuries with our own.

We had driven several miles when Peter broke the silence. "I'll never forget them," he said.

-31-

Throughout his ministry, Peter thought highly of the permanent deacons in the Catholic Church. He felt that they had an important ministry as married persons involved in the life of the parishes they served. These men were mature, usually married, devout Catholics who felt called to serve the Church in this ministry, while understanding that they would not be ordained priests. We made many friends among them and Peter supported them in their ministries.

We were close to one man in particular. Harry had never been assigned outside his home parish and suggested to Peter that he might like to work with him in Skiatook. Peter was delighted. Peter knew Harry well and thought he and his wife would be an asset to the parish as well as an invaluable assistant to Peter. He made the request to the bishop and who made the assignment in 1995.

"So you're getting a deacon out at Skiatook?" one of Peter's priest friends commented.

"Yes."

"Why do you want to do that to yourself?"

"What do you mean?"

"Some of us think they spy for the bishop. I haven't ever had one and I don't want one."

"Well, I don't have anything to hide from the bishop."

"Most of them just want to parade around the sanctuary. I can't see how they're useful."

"Any deacon who works for me will be a working deacon. I expect to have him running the educational program and working beside me with the people," Peter said.

As the weeks became months, Peter felt the increased pressure of trying to adjust to his lack of energy and the exhaustion that overtook him when he least expected it. He insisted that parish programs should continue as they had in the past, and yet given that he was involved in every aspect of parish life, I wondered how long he would be able to continue this way.

Harry and his wife had been a tremendous help in the parish and were with us when Peter became ill. We thought things were going fairly well until Harry seemed to lose interest in the work in Skiatook. He talked about wanting to work in one of the larger Tulsa parishes. His wife called frequently to say that he would not be able to come for Masses and events as planned. Then, in November 1997, she called to say that he would not be able to come at all that month.

Peter called the vicar general and tactfully suggested that he did not think Harry was happy in Skiatook, that he was frequently absent and that they might want to consider a transfer for him. He also suggested that Harry would be a good fit in the Tulsa parish he had said he would like to serve.

A few days later the bishop's secretary called to schedule a meeting with Peter at which the vicar general would also be present. When Peter went to the meeting, he learned that Deacon Harry had "tattled" as the other priest had predicted.

When Peter came home, he told me that his bishop wanted him to retire early.

"But you have to retire in May anyway because you'll be seventy years old," I said. "I don't understand. That's only six months away!"

"Harry told them that the parish is a mess."

"What? Didn't they want to hear what you had to say?"

"The vicar general was open to hearing me, but the bishop did not let either of us talk."

"Every person has a right to face his accuser. That's Biblical." I was furious. This sort of behavior had affected our lives far too many times in the Catholic Church.

"Apparently, I have no right of defense. Or explanation, in this case. Oh, Harry said a number of things. Like I encourage non-Catholics to receive communion."

"That's crazy. You have a notice in the bulletin that only Catholics in good standing may receive Holy Communion."

"I've never in my entire ministry had open communion. Not in the Episcopal, nor the Catholic Church." Peter shook his head. "He also said that I handle the Blessed Sacrament in an irreverent way. He said that I pour the consecrated wine down the sink and into the sewer."

"That's crazy. He should know that the sink in the sacristy is designed to drain directly into the ground, and not into the sewer system. Why didn't Harry bring these concerns to you?"

"Harry had asked me about this and I talked to Father Jim White, who said that even though the sink is set up to dispose of the Blessed Sacrament, it should be drunk so I told the Eucharistic ministers at that time that if they didn't want to consume the consecrated wine, I would do it."

Peter continued, "Harry also said that people are leaving the parish in droves."

"Where's he been anyway? He knows that some have left, but others have come in their place. The Church is full every Sunday. Why even the balcony seating is full."

"It's his word against mine and the bishop is taking his."

"When I think of all the times people complained about Harry and I defended him— They did not like his homilies. The Sunday school teachers would not work with him. I guess their instincts were right."

"Well, he also said that I am too lenient with divorced persons. I admit I am sympathetic to them. However, I have acted within canon law and I do not regret my decisions. I sought advice from a canon lawyer each time. The people I have counseled are older people who had short first marriages—often under tragic circumstances—and who have been in second marriages for years. They have come to Mass faithfully without receiving the sacraments. I still believe I did the right thing."

"Oh dear."

"I told the Bishop that divorced Catholics are the lepers of our church. The Church needs to meet them where they are with the greatest sensitivity possible. God knows, I don't encourage divorce."

"Now what's going to happen?"

"As I said, I'm going to retire the first of the year."

"I guess it's a good thing we have that house in Tulsa."

As long as I live, I thought, I would never be able to accept the politics of the Catholic Church. That our bishop would take the word of a deacon over one of his priests without so much as a question was unthinkable to me. I thought of the priest who said that the deacons were the bishop's spies. Obviously, he was not paranoid, nor was he exaggerating.

"I don't understand," I said. "Why would Harry say those things?"

"You know how they are. I think the bishop got him in there and cornered him, and Harry thought his own reputation was in question for some reason."

I felt stunned by Harry's actions. "I just can't believe he would do this. You were so good to him. You included him in every aspect of parish life. You shared your ministry with him. You gave him money for travel expenses. You bought him every vestment he requested. We had dinner for them nearly every week and sometimes twice a week, or we took them out. There was never a priest so good to a deacon." I shook my head.

"They said that Harry put it all in writing," Peter said.

"In writing? I would not have left that office without a copy of it. It's nothing less than slander. Do you realize that?"

"Mary, just calm down. It's small-minded, I'll grant you that."

"Did he ask you about your health?"

"No."

"I am so sick and tired of the hierarchy in the Catholic Church."

I wanted to get on with our lives. Now that the bishop had succeeded in casting a cloud over Peter's ministry, I wanted peace.

Sadly, I had almost come to expect this lack of professional maturity in so many of the priests and bishops.

"No matter what they do, it's still God's Church. I'll talk to Dr. Wolf, the president of the parish council, but I think the last Sunday in December will be our last Sunday here."

"Fine with me."

I was angry. Peter had worked with Harry in good faith, giving his support to Harry's ministry and expecting, indeed deserving, Harry's support in return. A man whom we thought was a friend had betrayed us.

When Peter wrote to the bishop saying that the last Sunday in December would be his final day in Skiatook, the Bishop did not reply. Instead, the vicar general sent a letter stating that the bishop would like Peter's last Mass to be Sunday, January 11th.

Surprised by this change, Peter asked, "I wonder why?"

"Don't you see? It's because the priests and the bishop leave on their vacations right after Christmas and he doesn't want to be inconvenienced by having to find a priest to take Mass here?"

I'll never forget Peter's sad smile. "Of course. You're absolutely right."

Peter did not want it known in the parish that his bishop had asked him to retire early and he wanted to protect the congregation from harboring any more bad feelings toward Deacon Harry. He simply wanted to retire quietly from his ministry. It was embarrassing and unnecessary, an open wound for both of us.

"Aren't you going to call Deacon Harry?" I asked while I cooked supper one evening.

"Why would I do that?" Peter responded.

"This could all be the result of a simple misunderstanding, or something..." My voice faded. "How could I think it was a misunderstanding?" I asked, amazed at my own need for a tangible answer.

"Mary, there's no misunderstanding. He knows exactly what he did."

"Could it be that you were set up by the Bishop?" I smiled. This didn't seem true either.

Peter's eyes met mine. "Mary...."

"Well I can't live with this open sore. I think we need to do something."

"I don't think we should talk to him. It would only end in anger and bitterness." Peter went to the counter to get the teapot. He poured another cup of tea and sat down at the table.

I said, "I can't live with unresolved issues. It will eat at me and I'll be angry until it is resolved in some way. I guess I just need some closure."

"Maybe we could write him a short letter to say that we don't understand why he did this to us, but we forgive him."

"That would certainly be better than nothing."

"The trouble is, we don't know why he did this or how I threatened and offended him."

"We can say that in the letter or note. I'll write it and you can approve. Okay?"

"Okay."

We wrote Deacon Harry a brief note.

He did not respond.

We learned that Deacon Harry had been assigned to the Tulsa parish that he had said he would like to serve.

On December 1, 1997, Peter mailed a letter to the congregation telling them of his retirement, announcing it in person at all the Masses the following Sunday. Some people were concerned that his early retirement meant that his health had rapidly deteriorated. We tried to assure them that this was not the case, without actually saying that the Bishop had asked him to retire five months early.

While we did not encourage it, several people wrote to the bishop to say that they appreciated our ministry and did not understand why Peter had to leave and retire early. Others wrote complimentary letters to the *Eastern Oklahoma Catholic*. They wanted to send a letter of support signed by everyone in the congregation to the bishop. Peter asked them not to. However, they did send one later.

The weeks passed too quickly, and before we knew it, Peter had celebrated his last Christmas Eve Mass at Sacred Heart Church. The little Christmas pageant angels, dressed in new gowns and wings sewn by Eileen Barnes, an angel herself, sang "Silent Night" and "Away in a Manger." Parents laughed and cried and I breathed a sigh of relief, that though the pageant was not perfect, it was filled with the joy of the Christ child.

On our last Sunday, the Altar Society hosted a beautiful dinner for us and many people came from St. Joseph Church in Hominy to say good-bye. There were cards, gifts, and good wishes. The Parish Council wanted to give Peter the church's Ford minivan but Peter declined, saying that it would serve the congregation better if it stayed in the parish.

Several of the Indian members of Sacred Heart presented Peter with a wool blanket of traditional Native American stripes on a red background, a gift to honor his ministry among them.

To my astonishment, Ginger Bennett, an Osage woman, presented me with an Indian shawl. I was deeply touched. My eyes filled with tears when Ginger wrapped the beautiful fringed purple shawl around my shoulders. She hugged me and said, "Thank you for all you have done for us."

I thought of these valiant Native Americans, the cruelty and tragedy of many of their experiences. Of all that they had overcome in their lives. And, yes, all that they had given those around them through their examples of courage and faithfulness. The I-Lon-Shka where I witnessed the dignity with which the Indians entered the pavilion. The drummers and singers. The dancers. Indian women wearing their beautiful shawls, dancing around and around the circle. Their feet cradled in soft leather moccasins. In my mind, I saw the three kings, the elders of the Osage, the Pottawatomie and the Shawnee. The eyes of the children on that first Epiphany Sunday.

I saw Marian struggling to play the organ at St. Jude Church, Rosalie, beside her, encouraging her. In my mind, I saw the death of a child and heard the wailing of Native American mourners. I heard Peter talking to the Indian woman at the dialysis center: "You must take care of yourself, Peggy." She had replied, "Father, I won't die if you're not here to bury me."

I saw the old woman, an amputee in a wheelchair, living alone in poverty in a mansion built decades ago with oil money, now lost for some inexplicable reason. Still, it was her home.

I could not help but feel that in a certain sense we were deserting them. Their lives would go on, not so different from what they were during our time with them. Other priests would come and go. It would all be the same, but we would no longer be a part of it.

This chapter of our journey had come to a close.

When the announcement of Peter's retirement appeared in the *Eastern Oklahoma Catholic*, it stated that he had retired for reasons of ill health, as did the letter the bishop wrote to all the priests. Although the mail brought numerous letters of support and appreciation to Peter from priests, he received no letter from his bishop thanking him for his service, as was the Bishop's custom.

During our ministry at St. Jude Church, Peter revitalized the parish, putting it on a stable financial footing.

At St. Joseph Church in Hominy, he established business practices to stabilize the congregation. He incorporated Native American spirituality into liturgical services and social functions. He encouraged the learning of and appreciation for Osage customs. Peter established community outreach through his participation in activities and the forming of a youth soccer club with the Methodist minister. He cooperated with the Osage Nation Social Services staff to improve the lives of the people.

The facilities at St. Joseph Church were improved during Peter's ministry there; the building was painted and a new metal roof installed. The rundown trailer home that had served as the rectory was sold and moved from the property.

The improvements at Sacred Heart Church in Skiatook were numerous beginning with appropriate authorization by Bishop Beltran to restore the name to Sacred Heart. During our time there, new carpeting replaced the three "make-do" pieces of carpet in the church. The cluttered balcony was cleared out, carpet installed and suitable seating arranged. A suitable, private confessional was built in the back of the church. The uneven, broken concrete entrance to the church was replaced. The small unlivable house west of the church, used as Peter's first office was sold and moved out and a concrete parking lot was poured.

In the rectory, the Altar Society replaced the kitchen appliances with a new gas range and electric refrigerator. They removed the rotting floor in the downstairs bathroom/laundry and replaced it.

During his ministry at Sacred Heart, Peter oversaw the building of a new wing on the parish hall. It consisted of a priest's office, secretary's office, and a formal meeting room. The parking lot around the hall was enlarged and extended to accommodate the number of parishioners.

Program-wise, Peter established a parish council including representatives from each parish organization. He encouraged the men of the parish to be involved in the Men's Club and the Knights of Columbus. He directed a group of retired folks in making chocolate St. Nicholas' for the feast day. They sold them to other parishes and he offered them to Catholic schools for a reduced price and sometimes free. He encouraged community outreach, participating in the ministerial alliance. He and the Emanuel Baptist Church minister exchanged pulpits. He gave the WWII veterans a place to meet once a month. Peter established a Sea Explorer Ship where all teens in the community were welcome. This was done with the assistance of laymen in the parish and the Oklahoma National Guard. He held a weekly teen study program called Pizza with Father Pete.

Peter gave office space one day a week to WIC (a food distribution program for Women, Infants and Children) in our education building. Native Americans came to Sacred Heart parish hall for their food commodities. Peter said that they could only meet there if they served coffee, cookies and heated or cooled the building depending on the weather. He never charged rent to any charitable outreach program. He felt that it was the church's responsibility and privilege to serve the poor and disenfranchised.

The rectory was always open to anyone who needed help or just wanted to talk.

It was an unusually good and happy life.

Father Peter celebrates Mass in the home of a parishioner in Skiatook.

-32-

Tulsa, Oklahoma

1998

Although we lived with the constant presence of Peter's myeloma, we thanked God that he had given us the gift of this time to share. Each time Peter saw Dr. Browning and the blood tests remained relatively stable, we grew in confidence that "no treatment was the best treatment". We enjoyed our newly remodeled 1920s home and the fun of creating a beautiful backyard to enjoy with friends. Within a short time, I had settled into a satisfying routine. Still, it felt like the sand in the hourglass of our lives was running out. Always present was the fear that his next doctor's appointment would deliver the dreadful news that the cancer had started to grow again. I never asked why it had stopped growing; it was a gift and most certainly the answer to prayers, and perhaps especially those of Pope John Paul II.

"I can't tell you what it means to me to have time to read and study without the pressure of parish responsibilities," Peter said, opening the screen door to the deck and joining me with his morning tea and a book.

With springtime upon us, it had become my habit to take the morning paper and my breakfast to the deck. I often remained there to write as well. The early mornings in Tulsa were comfortably cool, even in mid-summer. By ten o'clock, it would be too hot and humid outdoors for me. Most evenings brought a soft breeze and the yard would become pleasant again.

"I'm glad you're enjoying this time," I said. "I was afraid you wouldn't have enough to do."

Even after years of active ministry, with a brief interlude for academic preparation and testing to become a Catholic priest, the sudden lack of responsibility and direction did not weigh heavily on Peter. He kept a busy, disciplined schedule, filling his days with Mass, scripture study, prayer and meditation. Then an afternoon swim at St. John Health Club where he met old friends and made new ones. He went daily to Adoration, an hour in prayer in the presence of the Blessed Sacrament. Two afternoons a week, he celebrated Mass for the Benedictine Sisters at St. Joseph Monastery, and occasionally he said Mass for parishes in the area, but for the most part, he kept to himself and enjoyed the solitude.

A short time after Peter retired, he found he did not have the stamina to go out to parishes that required driving and staying over night. Therefore, he made the decision to substitute only in the Tulsa area. The privilege of celebrating Mass for the Sisters meant a great deal to him. He had been hurt by the Bishop's actions and he welcomed the restoration of his dignity by serving the Sisters whom he loved and respected.

One day at the monastery, Sister Barbara, the Prioress said, "Mary, it's so generous of Father Peter to celebrate Mass for us." She laughed when she added, "Sister Joachim thinks we're doing it for him."

"You *are* doing it for him. It means so much to him to come here, and he does need it. I'm so glad you invite him," I said.

To myself, I marveled at how these women had been a constant in our lives. Sister Joachim was a wise older nun who intuitively grasped the inner workings of the Church. Throughout our years in Tulsa, when Peter needed support the most, the sisters instinctively included us in their Benedictine life, without any sense of creating a place to accommodate us. With them, we felt welcomed and loved.

I found that my work at the medical college was less burdensome after Peter retired. Though I had not minded the commute from Skiatook, it was good to be relieved of it and my parish responsibilities. Now I came home each evening to the simple demands of dinner and household chores, and my evenings were restful and refreshing.

I wanted to return to a more disciplined writing schedule on my second book, but I remained the victim of writer's block. The small group of priests who had attacked me after the release of my first book had effectively shut me down. How could I get out of this pit and move on? Each time I sat down at my computer keyboard or snuggled into my favorite armchair with pad and pencil, those same priests seemed to look over my shoulder and judge every word I wrote, figuratively speaking of course. I could not put a meaningful sentence on the page. I continued to feel caught in the same devious web of self-conscious fear I had experienced in the years after my first book. This small group of priests had silenced me and I simply could not write without the incessant meddling of my inner editor.

I thought about taking a creative writing class and explored various possibilities. I chose a night class at Oklahoma State University, feeling that it might be a good challenge. I knew that Teresa Miller, the instructor, was a novelist, but this would be my first exposure to her in the classroom.

Teresa's teaching method was to give almost no criticism, but simply to encourage and reinforce each writer's gifts. Initially I felt both frustrated and encouraged. I felt that my writing skills were not improving.

I gradually realized that the way Teresa taught writing was to allow her students freedom to create. I relaxed, listened to her, and realized that she was working on my inner editor by giving me the confidence I longed for. I learned that it was not important what I wrote, but simply that I wrote. The rest would come.

Out of that class, six of us formed a critique group. Since most of us worked during the day, we met at a restaurant on Fridays for lunch and talk. Because our meetings were short, we brought our manuscripts to the meeting; each person took a copy home and brought them back the following week with penciled-in remarks. At each meeting, we discussed the work from the previous week. It was extremely effective and we formed a bond of encouragement and friendship.

More than anything else, I was grateful to be writing again and working toward my goal of a memoir.

In June 1998, the bishop appointed a priest to be pastor of Sacred Heart Church in Skiatook. The priest called and asked to meet with us. The parish had been without a pastor for more than five months. A priest from a neighboring parish had been the administrator, and various priests had filled in for weekend Masses. None of them contacted Peter about parish life or programs there. We wondered why the new pastor wanted to see us.

When he arrived, he asked questions about the congregation and parish programs. We were pleased to tell him of our rich experiences there and our admiration for the people. He stood to go and said, "I was told that the place was a mess, disorganized and poorly managed. However, I have not found that to be true in the short time I've been there. You did a good job, Peter."

His words were heartwarming and gratifying. We knew that rumors and stories had spread throughout the Diocese; we assumed they were largely due to Deacon Harry's reporting. We felt indebted to this priest for his kind words. Although our bishop had not recognized the work Peter had accomplished there, this man knew the truth of our ministry and that was enough for us.

-33-

The bright flashes of lightning through the thin veil of my eyelids stirred me from a sound sleep, and I awakened to hear the first heavy drops of rain hit the roof over our bedroom. Oklahoma weather—what did Will Rogers say. "If you don't like the weather, stick around a minute; it'll change." I loved the exciting rush of wind and the downpour of warm spring rain—the tornado warnings. Then it's over and we awaken to the clean fresh air of a sunny morning. So much a part of this Oklahoma life.

I turned toward Peter. He wrapped his arms around me. On the roof, the rain beat out the rhythm of this new springtime.

"Time to get going." I rolled out of bed and headed for the kitchen and fresh coffee.

Alone in my study, later that morning, I asked God to bless my meditation. I asked myself the question: If this were the last day of my life, how would I spend it? As I wrote the question in my notebook, it gained new meaning for me. I thought seriously about it, as I had never felt a need to in the past. What will I do on this last day of my life?

Most of all I would want to be with Peter. Just be with him. I would call my children and tell them how much I cherish who they are. That I would like to have lived near them and really known them and their worlds. That I wish we had more time together; that our lives had been less cluttered with meaningless trivia. On this last day, I would tell them that I love them and honor them, that their lives have filled mine with meaning and joy.

On this last day then, I would ask Peter to sit with me and share our last moments together. I would try to find the words to tell him what his love has meant to me. That through him I've been able to grow. That he has given me the freedom to be myself, the soul that God created me to be and that through his strength and personality, and God's grace, I have been nurtured and fulfilled by our marriage vows and the ministry we have shared.

Our talks about death have begun to come easily. We have become unselfconscious growing together, learning to face this newest challenge. It is amazing to me that our talk moves easily from life, pain and death to simple things. Perhaps these are life's only realities.

We had planned to escape the Oklahoma summer heat and return to Washington where we would spend a couple of weeks at the Sixes Ranch cabin on the Oregon Coast. Peter had been having more pain than usual. He felt apprehensive about the trip and the possibility of being ill, especially while having our grandchildren, Paul and Caitlin with us, but we decided to go anyway.

We arrived in Seattle, and our son, John, met us at the airport. We took him out to lunch and picked up the Ford minivan at Hertz. John came home that evening with a King salmon for dinner. It was fresh out of the water and delicious. I wished that everyone I knew in Tulsa could share this incredible seafood and the light sea breezes of Puget Sound. As long as we lived in Tulsa, I had been painfully aware of the change in air quality each time we arrived at Sea-Tac Airport and again when we deplaned in Tulsa. By contrast, the air in Tulsa was heavy and humid. That evening, enjoying the cool breeze off Puget Sound while we ate fresh salmon in John and Sherry's back yard I thanked God for giving us the means to make this trip every summer.

The next morning we helped Paul, now twelve years old, and Caitlin, nine, pack for the drive down the coast. We arrived at the cabin after dark, tired and ready for hot chocolate and a bedtime story.

I loved sunrise at the cabin. At first light, I sat with my cup of coffee and watched the mouth of the river, hoping that Paul and Caitlin would sleep late and I would have these hours of solitude. The sounds of their deep breathing floated in peaceful rhythms from the loft. As the light seeped westward over the coastal hills, the trees were silhouetted against the sky, and in the distance the dark outline of Castle Rock revealed itself.

I thought of Paul and Caitlin, who said they could not remember a summer when they did not come to the cabin with us. They have grown a foot or more since we last saw them and Paul is stretching his personality as well, finding out who he is and where the boundaries lie. Both bright and energetic, I hope they will always believe that they can accomplish anything they set their minds to. As I thought of their young lives, the light deepened and Castle Rock appeared to be sitting topless in the thick morning fog so common on the coast. Outside the cabin, a flock of swallows swooped and dove under and around the eaves. Theirs was a kind of frenzy and I wondered if our sudden appearance had somehow threatened their way of life.

The tide was low that morning and I saw a family of raccoons catching their breakfast of fresh trout at the waters edge. Soon a blue heron joined them—we had seen one each of the past three summers here. As the wind came up and the fog around Castle Rock moved out to sea, I heard movement above me in the loft.

Then, Paul said, "Grandma Mary, are we going to have pancakes for breakfast?"

My quiet time had ended. It was our first day at the cabin and there were important things to do and see.

"Is the Pope Catholic?" I asked. "Of course we're going to have pancakes."

That was the first year that Peter had difficulty walking the mile or so to the beach. The myeloma had depleted his strength and it was for these small things that we found we grieved the most. We spent a lot of time in the cabin reading and watching movies on television. We played dominoes and made popcorn and s'mores, the children's favorite dessert snack.

Satiated with cool coastal breezes and gentle sun, we left our grandchildren at home in Seattle and returned to Tulsa. As always, the impact of the Oklahoma summer heat and humidity hit us square in the face as we stepped through the revolving doors leaving the air-conditioned airport terminal behind. I longed for the next weeks to pass quickly, to move on to September and October, when Oklahoma dresses herself in vibrant shades of orange and gold, and gentle breezes send fallen leaves dancing down the street in front of our house.

Oklahoma summer evenings were rarely comfortable enough to have the front door open with only the screen door to shield us from the squadron of flying insects. Early in the spring we turned on the air conditioning the same day we shut off the heat, the reverse happened in the fall. The summer found us living our lives indoors and avoiding outdoor gatherings. Already, as I had every year since coming to Oklahoma, I dreaded the next summer, nearly a year in the future.

Oklahoma winters, though short, are dry and brown. For this green-loving West Coaster, the bright winter sun made the drab landscape bearable. I often bought cut flowers and flowering plants at the market to have garden color in the house, if not outdoors. I had hoped that the short winters would grow on me and I frequently reminded myself that short winters were far better than the long months of low hanging clouds and drizzling rains of the Pacific Northwest. Still, for me, the winters dragged in spite of their brevity.

That fall we talked about a possible return move to Washington State. Unspoken between us was the fact that we had been reluctant to leave our children and grandchildren when our summer vacation ended. Unlike the ministry in which we had lived wherever the Church, Episcopal or Catholic, sent us, we were now free to live wherever we chose.

Retirement should be a time to satisfy personal needs. When we came to Oklahoma we expected to finish out our lives here, but as the years passed we longed to be near our children and extended family.

Yet I felt ambivalent about such a move. Peter's health was a factor. We liked his doctors in Tulsa where he received excellent medical care. We would have the task of finding new ones in the Seattle area. On the plus side, we would have the support of our children if we lived nearer to them.

There were days, too, when it seemed that the pain and stiffness in my joints would make such a move extremely difficult. I wondered if I was up to it physically. If not now, would I ever be able to move back? Moreover, if something happened to Peter here, would I be able to move alone?

Then there was our house. To consider selling it after we had put so much of ourselves into the remodeling project felt like a betrayal.

It was Saturday afternoon and Peter stood at the door to my study where I was working on some notes for my book.

I said, "I love this house and we've worked so hard on it. And this yard. I've always wanted a back yard with tall trees." I looked around at the changes we had made, the furnishings we had carefully selected, expecting to remain here the rest of our days. "And our friends, people who have supported us and your priesthood. We would have to leave them behind. I know that it would not be the same in Washington."

I thought of my friends on Vashon Island; of how leaving had left me with an emptiness that had taken years to fill. How I would love to renew those friendships, at the same time knowing that they would not be the same if we returned.

"When do you retire from the college?" he asked.

"Next year. July 1st."

"That gives us almost a year to think about it and make decisions."

"It's a big step to consider," I said.

We both became silent, each absorbed in our own thoughts.

I remembered again the rainy day in 1983 when we loaded our suitcases and a few kitchen necessities into our old Dodge station wagon to leave Vashon Island for Oklahoma. It was one of those wonderfully moist September mornings when the leaves are still on the trees and the fall air is not chilly yet. At the end of the driveway, I looked back. I did not regret leaving our two-story Tudor cottage. We had raised our children here. We were leaving the house, but we would always have our memories.

I recalled driving onto the ferry, ecstatic that at last this exciting adventure in the Catholic Church had begun. Then I thought of our trip back to the Island two years later. How we stopped to visit the folks who bought the house, and I burst into tears when I walked into the living room. They had chosen the same oriental pattern and color of rug that we had bought from

Sears when we lived there. They had not seen our rug, and they could not have known that they had duplicated it.

Peter interrupted my thoughts. "You're off somewhere else aren't you?"

I smiled. "Yes, I guess I am." I looked out our window in Tulsa and saw the two backyard squirrels chasing each other, one scolding while the other scampered to a higher limb.

I turned to Peter. "I think we could get our money out of this house, but what about things like the porch swing that Vern Jones made for me? I don't know if I would have a place to use it. They don't have big porches in the West like they do here, only decks and patios."

"Those decisions can be made later," Peter assured me. "It's sure going to cost us one heckuva lot to move."

-34-

In April, we placed a for-sale sign in our front yard. Imagine our surprise when we sold the house within hours. Having expected to have several months to show the house and finalize the sale, we faced immediate yard sales and the need for temporary short-term housing. We were in shock.

May, June and July of 2001 run together in my memory. When a yard sale is also a moving sale there is a county fair feeling to the event. I've always been more of a gift-giver than a sales person, and I found a lot of joy in simply offering certain furniture or other items to a friend or neighbor whom I knew needed them. I did not mind downsizing again. I had done it when we moved to Tulsa and I knew that while some things were difficult to part with, when it was over, I would again feel free and far less burdened by possessions I didn't need or could do without. Through my own experience, I could certainly see the wisdom and joy of holy poverty: a life of simplicity with focus and meaning at its core.

Two weeks after we sold the house, we stepped into a beautiful Seattle springtime. The bright sunlight and scent of flowering cherry trees on the light coastal breeze played upon my imagination. In my heart, I felt like singing and dancing down the street, but instead I took Peter's hand, inviting him to walk with me through our son's West Seattle neighborhood.

As we neared Alki Point, the deep blue of Puget Sound waters reflected against the sky and we heard the voices of children and teens playing on the beach. The air felt light, fresh, and clean. I breathed deeply, closed my eyes, and held it all within. Yes, this is home, I thought. We belong here.

We made John's house our base of operations while we looked at too many homes to count or remember in West Seattle. We could not find anything within our budget that did not need enlarging or at least substantial remodeling. Our realtor mentioned that houses were more reasonably priced in Olympia, an hour south of Seattle. I had dreamed of being near our son and his family in order to be more involved with Paul and Caitlin, but perhaps south Puget Sound would do.

In Olympia, we found an attractive condominium with a panoramic view of the Capitol and the Black Hills in the distance. Since it was only three blocks from St. Michael Catholic Church, we decided to make an offer on the property.

"I've said it before but this is just about the last place I expected to live." I laughed.

"I know you wanted to be closer to the kids, but it is a nice little community and the condo is really the only place we've looked at that is suitable and near a Catholic church," Peter said.

"And there are lots of lakes and parks in the area with hiking trails and camping facilities."

"Remember, the earthquake a month ago? Six point eight on the Richter scale? It was centered a few miles from here in the Nisqually Delta." We had seen telltale signs of damage around town.

"Yes, but that's like saying that tornadoes are centered in Tulsa. Earthquakes happen all the time up and down the coast."

"I've never been bothered by minor earthquakes. Do you remember how our house on Vashon Island used to shake with little quakes? Especially upstairs." I laughed. The truth was I had begun to see possibilities for an interesting life in Olympia. "I have to admit that it is a tremendous relief to find a nice home that we can afford."

"Let's find out what time Mass is tomorrow."

In our room, I looked in the yellow pages of the telephone book. There were two Catholic churches: St. Michael and Sacred Heart, and I noticed something else. "Peter, did you know there is a Byzantine Catholic Church here?"

"I knew there was one somewhere between Seattle and Portland, but I didn't know it was here."

"It's on the Yelm Highway and there is a Divine Liturgy this evening."

"How close are we to the church?"

"I don't know, but we can ask at the front desk."

When Peter inquired, he learned that we were not far from the church. The receptionist gave us driving directions and said that we should be able to reach it in time for the evening liturgy.

When we arrived at St. George, the parking lot was empty. We walked to the back of the property where we saw an outdoor pavilion. A pick-up truck drove into the parking lot and a young man got out and walked toward us.

"This is a shrine to Our Lady of Perpetual Help," he explained. "But, it's not finished. We are getting ready to install the beautiful mosaic icon in a couple of weeks."

He offered his hand to Peter and said, "I'm Pat Norton. There is no Divine Liturgy tonight. Our priest had eye surgery today and couldn't come. Something told me that I needed to drive over here on the chance that someone might be here who didn't know the Liturgy was canceled."

"No liturgy," Peter said. "Will there be one tomorrow morning?"

"No. Our priest lives in Seattle and won't be down. Are you new here?"

"I'm Father Peter Dally and this is my wife, Mary. I'm a retired priest from Tulsa, Oklahoma." Peter carefully explained his background and the special circumstances through which he was ordained.

"We just made an offer on a condominium this afternoon," I said.

"Did you know we have a monastery here?"

"No," Peter said.

"Yup. We have two nuns just down the road. Holy Theophany Community. I'd like to take you to meet them if you have time."

"If we're not disturbing them," Peter said.

We followed Pat Norton's red truck to the monastery where we met Sisters Anastasia and Irene. Sister Anastasia told us that a priest visiting from Australia would celebrate the Divine Liturgy in their chapel the following morning. She invited us to return and have breakfast with them afterward. We accepted.

These Eastern Christians have welcomed us with their hospitality and warmth, I thought to myself. Their congregations have married priests in Europe. Only hours had passed since making the offer on the condo and already it seemed that we had chosen the wrong Catholic church to live near. Intuitively I knew that these people would accept us and I wondered if we would be as welcome at St. Michael Church. However, I did not tell Peter about the uneasiness that gnawed at me.

We returned to Tulsa where I would work until my retirement in July. We said good-bye to our many friends in Tulsa. Difficult good-byes should be short. However, our good-byes lingered and resonated over weeks that dragged and pulled us back into life in Tulsa. People were gracious and wanted to do many things for us and it grew harder and harder to pull away and embrace the inevitability of leaving them behind.

The pastor and our friends at Sacred Heart Church in Skiatook invited us to come for Mass and dinner, a final farewell. He asked Peter to give the homily, and Peter was pleased to preach to the people one last time, recalling stories and incidents from our years with them.

At the dinner after Mass, I looked across the room and I thought of all the ways these people had honored me, the first priest's wife they had had, and likely to be the only priest's wife. There was Vern Jones, a man whose professional life had ended when he lost a leg in a tragic automobile accident, only to become a skilled wood craftsman. He had hand crafted the handsome new altar for the church, not to mention several personal gifts for us. I watched the children I had taught in the first communion class. They had grown so much. In another year I wouldn't recognize them—striking and beautiful, every one of them. The day was full of rich memories.

Even the Sea Explorer unit that Peter had sponsored came to mind when I happened to look over the heads of two matronly women seated across from me, to see a tiny hole, then another one—BBs gone astray during marksmanship practice. I smiled to myself. What a trial those boys were—too much for Peter after he became ill. I wondered what had happened to them in the time since the group disbanded. Many faced huge challenges and life issues that had to be overcome for a healthy future.

This saying good-bye and moving on to a new life reminded me of one spring morning as I sat in my car in south Tulsa. A monarch butterfly alighted on the windshield. Then hundreds more joined it. Soon masses of beautiful monarch butterflies swarmed around me. I knew that a few days earlier these same monarchs had been in the chrysalis stage, worm-like creatures wrapped in the protection of miniature cocoons. Then something magical happened and they entered this vast and tumultuous world in a new and even more wondrous life as a fluttering creature of beauty.

I knew that in leaving Oklahoma to return to the Northwest, I was leaving something precious. Here, in this city, we had experienced God in a new way through Peter's priesthood. We found and accepted warm friendships at every turn. These Okies, whom we loved and respected, would always be a part of us and I felt sure that in some small way we would remain a part of them.

Our life in Washington would be a metamorphosis of sorts. Requiring yet another chrysalis stage. Another rebirth. Like the monarch butterfly, I hoped that we could face this newest transition with grace, that our new life would be one of beauty and peace.

I finished my work at the medical college and said good-bye to my friends there. It was yet another tearing away, a wrenching that I had hoped we would not have to make, and yet, when the time came, I knew we must.

We arrived in Olympia, Washington on a Saturday night. The next day was Sunday and Peter asked me, "Where do you want to go to Mass? We could have a simple Mass here in our hotel room or would you like to go to St. Michael?"

"I want to wait for John and his family to get to our condo and then I'd like you to celebrate Mass in our new home," I said.

"Oh? We won't have our furniture moved in yet."

"All we need is a small table, and you can use your portable Mass kit."

"All right. I think that would be very nice."

The next morning John, Sherry, Paul, and Caitlin and their friend Brad Baller met us at the condominium. We gathered in the living room and Peter blessed the house and celebrated Mass. It meant a lot to me that this family worship was the first event in our new home. I listened to Caitlin read the Epistle and watched Paul serve the altar for his grandfather. This home may not be down the street or even in the same neighborhood as my grandchildren, but today we had made a memory for all of us. It was a new beginning. I thought once again of the Monarch butterflies. I wondered at the mystery of their short lives, the worm-like bodies stretching to open tiny cocoons, and then emerging in recreated beauty, fantastical beings to thrill and delight those who would open their eyes to see.

-35-

Peter wrote to the archbishop in Seattle, explaining his situation as a Pastoral Provision priest retired from the Diocese of Tulsa. He said that if the archbishop agreed he would be willing to assist at St. Michael Church in Olympia or wherever he was needed on a part-time temporary basis. The archbishop responded with a warm letter saying that he was certain he could use him. He asked Peter to telephone his assistant to make an appointment to discuss where he could fit in.

When Peter telephoned the assistant's office, he explained to the bishop's secretary that the archbishop had asked him to call and make an appointment to meet with his assistant. When Peter did not receive a return call, he called a second time. Again, he was not able to speak to the bishop, and the secretary said he would call back to schedule an appointment.

Neither the secretary nor the assistant bishop responded to Peter's telephone calls as the archbishop's letter had specified.

I refused to feel bitter about the lack of courtesy. I am sad to say that I almost expected it, so cynical had I become with regard to the Catholic Church. Yet, I thought, I must remember the many Godly people—priests, sisters, and laypersons—who supported us and nurtured us throughout this twenty-year journey in faith. It was too easy to let the sad experiences dominate my thoughts and opinions of the Catholic Church. Still, Peter was a priest and he deserved courtesy from a Catholic bishop, any Catholic bishop. Once again, it did not seem to me that the Catholic hierarchy recognized the concept of a sacramental priesthood, for if they did, they would support the Holy Father and the Pastoral Provision.

Peter requested a meeting with the pastor at St. Michael Church. We both thought the situation could be remedied when the pastor would clear it up with the archbishop. We learned that the pastor was on sabbatical and would return in the late fall.

Each Sunday we went to the Divine Liturgy at St. George Byzantine Catholic Church. We were familiar with this rite because our friend, Father Gary Sherman, founded a Byzantine congregation in Tulsa. There, the relationship between the Latin Rite—sometimes referred to as Roman Rite or Western Rite—and the other Catholic rites—Byzantine, Maronite, Melkite, and Tridentine—is congenial and cooperative. Articles and liturgy schedules for these rites appeared in the *Eastern Oklahoma Catholic* newspaper on a regular basis, and it is a widely accepted fact that they are all under the Holy Father. All Catholics are in communion regardless of the "incidentals" of their liturgical practices.

Eastern Rite Catholics most often have their origins in Eastern Europe. Located geographically in close proximity to the Ottoman Empire—which lasted from the 13th century until the end of World War I—the countries of Eastern Europe are significantly influenced by the people of Greece and Turkey. The Byzantine rite, also known as Ruthenian originated in Slavic countries. Maronites and Melkites originate in Lebanon. Tridentine refers to the traditional form of the Latin Mass. It is not widely known by American Catholics that there are more than twenty different rites within the Roman Catholic Church. While small in numbers compared to the large congregations in the Latin Rite, these groups are not heretical or schismatic, but Catholic in every sense. Nevertheless, together, we are all Catholics under the Pope, and Tulsa Catholics welcomed the diversity. Seasonal celebrations and customs reflect the character and makeup of their cultural origins. Many beautiful Eastern customs have been adapted for use in our Latin Rite parishes. One such custom is the observance of the Feast of Saint Nicholas on December 6th.

We were stunned to learn that in the Archdiocese of Seattle, the Latin Rite and the Byzantine Rite do not enjoy the cooperation and supportive relationships that we had experienced in Tulsa. Sadly, strained dealings and instances of false reporting characterized the association between the Latin and Byzantine Rites. For example, the Archdiocese did not post Divine Liturgy schedules for the Byzantine Rite congregations at Latin Rite parishes or in the diocesan newspaper. We were amazed that there was virtually no official cooperation between the two rites.

Even more shocking, some devout Catholics—who should have known better—told us that Byzantine Catholics are not Catholic at all.

It is a sad commentary on Christianity the world over that those who follow Jesus allow their differences to dominate their relationships with other Christians. However, it is far more tragic that Catholic people are not better informed and supportive of the various expressions within the Catholic Church.

We had met Father Joseph Stanichar, pastor at St. John Chrysostom Byzantine Catholic Church in Seattle, on our summer and holiday visits to the area. Peter talked to Father Joseph and Father Lee Perry, at St. George Church, about the possibility of obtaining Byzantine faculties so that he could assist or fill in when a substitute priest was needed in either parish. Both priests agreed that it would be a welcome luxury to have another priest available to supply for them.

The bishop of a diocese must license a priest if he is to celebrate the sacraments there. For the Byzantine Rite, this would be the Bishop of the Eparchy of Van Nuys, under whose jurisdiction the Washington parishes reside. Father Lee sponsored Peter's application to this end. Our bishop in Tulsa would need to approve the arrangement as well. None of this would change Peter's canonical status as a priest in the Diocese of Tulsa. He would be bi-ritual, meaning that he would be authorized to celebrate both the Latin Rite Mass and the Byzantine Rite Divine Liturgy.

St. George Byzantine Catholic Church, Olympia, Washington

Peter began a somewhat lengthy and demanding period of training to learn the Byzantine liturgy. We drove to Seattle every Monday to attend the Divine Liturgy at St. John Chrysostom where Peter met with Father Joseph. He also participated in the parish icon class under Judit Crow, a master iconographer.

It is correct to say that one writes—or paints—icons. The faithful revere these sacramentals as windows to heaven because each icon represents the saint as he or she appears in heaven and includes symbolism, colors, and lettering specific to the saint. The artist applies color from dark to light. In the Book of Genesis and in the first chapter of the Gospel of John, light enters into the darkness, symbolizing God's love and beauty. The iconographer prepares to write an icon by fasting and prayer because the icon itself is an instrument of prayer and worship from its conception throughout its creation and life. Heather Williams

Durka, a master iconographer, says, "My heart is in my hands. It's all about prayer."

While Peter attended the icon class, I was free to wander about Seattle and renew old friendships. I marveled at the changes I saw in the city, especially its parks and museums. Alki Point with its miles of beaches became a favorite place for me to walk and enjoy a coffee at Starbucks. The Public Market with its sights and smells was a wonderful place to shop, especially on a Monday when attendance was small. It was a joy, too, to meet old friends like Nicole Mertes, whom I had worked for in Tulsa, for long lunches. My Mondays in Seattle were mini-vacations that I looked forward to each week.

When the pastor at St. Michael Church returned after several months sabbatical, Peter made an appointment to meet with him and asked me to come along.

Peter explained to the pastor that the archbishop asked him to meet with his assistant bishop, but that he had not gotten past his secretary. Nor had the bishop returned his telephone call.

After the three of us talked about ways that he might help, Peter said, "I think that it would be good to explain to the people that I am married and a part of the Pastoral Provision. I don't think it would be good to just appear with a wedding band on my finger."

The other priest leaned back in his chair and appeared to withdraw into himself. "Oh...." He stroked his chin and with his free hand, clutched his notebook. I felt him "move" further from us. "I think that would cause too much trouble in the parish. I don't know...."

"If you don't tell them, they will wonder who I am and if I am really a priest," Peter said.

"We've always been easily accepted by lay people once they understand our situation." I smiled, hoping to encourage the pastor. "When Peter was assigned to the cathedral in Tulsa, the priest announced who he was, that he was married and explained the Pastoral Provision. We served Holy Family Cathedral for four years, and Peter had his own parish in a small town for seven years after that. We were warmly received by the people."

"I'd like to have the help, but I'm afraid it would cause too many problems," he said.

As we left the parish office, I said to Peter, "I would think he would at least discuss it with the archbishop."

"You're not surprised, are you?"

"Well, no, but I don't want to anticipate these sorts of rejections."

"How can we not?" Peter's voice filled with disappointment.

"I know, but I'd like to think that in twenty years there would be some growth in this archdiocese. He sounded like this was the first he'd thought about your being married."

"I made it clear from the beginning."

"I don't know why they think that telling the people causes problems. In our experience it prevents them."

"I can't put my mind in theirs. I don't know how they think."

After that meeting, Peter frequently attended daily Mass at St. Michael Church, but on Sundays, we drove twelve miles to St. George. Our relationship with Bishop William Skurla and the priests of the Byzantine Eparchy of Van Nuys was warm and genuine. Peter received his faculties to celebrate the Divine Liturgy within months. He then assisted and filled in for Father Lee whenever he was needed.

Peter never received faculties from the Archdiocese of Seattle.

These sorts of events, or non-events, are sad to me. In a reasonable world, whether a priest is married or not would not be an issue. We say that the Catholic Church's tradition is celibacy when that has not always been so. It was not until the Third Lateran Council in 1179 that Church law required celibacy of all priests and bishops in the Latin Rite. Over the years, I have come to feel that the Church tends to revise its history to suit the message it wishes to convey. For example, we do not say that all of the popes have been celibate; we simply do not say that some of them were married and had children. In fact, many priests and bishops in the early church were the sons of priests and bishops, and even popes.

Had there not been an ancient tradition in the Catholic Church of a married priesthood for more than a thousand years after Jesus' ascension, and if celibacy were not a law that came into being less than a thousand years ago, I might feel differently. I love my Church. It is the faith I have chosen. I can only pray that, for the sake of our people, reform will come and that celibacy will one day be an option for men entering the priesthood. It could happen with a "stroke of the pen."

Unwanted by the priest at St. Michael Church, we turned more fully to our Byzantine Catholic friends where once again we found a home with an order of religious women. Sister Anastasia and Sister Irene welcomed us warmly. After we had been there several months, their priest was no longer able to serve them and Peter stepped in to fill the need. Each Saturday we drove to the monastery where he celebrated the Divine Liturgy and we stayed for brunch and lively conversations. It became the highlight of our week.

Our condominium was beautiful, one of the nicest homes we had lived in. Still, we had become increasingly dissatisfied with it. And, Peter had not been able to help at St. Michael Church as he had hoped. St. George Church and the sisters had readily welcomed him. However, it was a twenty-four mile drive for him to attend the daily Divine Liturgy. It took most of the morning to drive there, participate in the service, and return home. If he were not feeling well enough to drive himself, I drove him. And I would do that, for I could not, and would not, deprive him of his desire and need to live out his priesthood, even in this small way. However, I theorized, if we lived near the Church he could drive himself and we could both be more independent. It seemed natural then that we should be thinking about moving closer to the two communities in which we had found our niche. Still, it seemed capricious to make another move simply for convenience' sake.

I thought of the evening we first visited St. George and met the Sisters at Holy Theophany. I remembered how I felt. The doubts that lingered after our decision to buy the condominium because it was near St. Michael Church. Even then, I knew the Byzantine Catholics would welcome us. However, naively, I felt confident that the archdiocese and St. Michael Church would receive us as well.

I recalled a letter I received from a leading Seattle priest after the publication of my first book. He apologized for the treatment we had received when Peter applied to the Pastoral Provision through the archdiocese of Seattle. The priest said that he hoped the archdiocese could welcome us back to the area one day, that he hoped there would be an opportunity to make up for the lack of charity we had experienced at that time. Sadly, that had not happened.

We sold our condominium for the asking price within a month and moved into our new one-level home on Indian Summer Drive. I had no doubts this time. Though it had been by way of a crooked path, the Holy Spirit had led us here and it felt right in every way. Our son, John, and the men at St. George Church helped us move, which minimized not only the labor, but also the expense.

Before we knew it, the disruption of the move was behind us and we settled into a comfortable routine. Life is good, I thought. Now we have only to enjoy our new home and each other.

-36-

The winter of 2002 was mild in Western Washington. We took our time to refurbish the dying landscape in front of our house and began work on the back yard. While we worked as though we had years to accomplish the needed changes, always present was the unspoken reality that Peter's time for wielding a pickaxe and shovel was limited. It was with a sense of pride and accomplishment that he designed and completed each area, preparing it for minimum maintenance. Springtime's promise of rebirth when evergreens we had planted sprouted new growth and rhododendrons budded and bloomed in an array of color, were answer enough for our efforts. It gave Peter particular satisfaction to realize that he could still manage this physical work. For me, there was sadness that this could be the last.

Peter's oncologist, Dr. Lorrin Yee's, quarterly tests consistently showed that the multiple myeloma continued to smolder, and so we relaxed, anticipating another summer of relative good health for him. We looked forward to the warmth of a gentle

Pacific Northwest sun and planned our annual pilgrimage to the ranch cabin at the mouth of the Sixes River in Oregon.

However, in May 2003 Peter's blood tests showed that the blood protein levels were rising, an indication that the myeloma had progressed. Dr. Yee recommended monthly zomata infusions to strengthen his bones and he began a protocol of forty milligrams of dexamethasone every seven days. Each week when he took this steroid, he became anxious and agitated and could not sleep for forty-eight hours. No sooner did he recover from these side effects than it was time to begin the exhausting cycle all over again. This was a trying time for both of us as we wondered if the side effects of this drug were worth the beneficial qualities.

Needing a break from the stress, a friend invited me to go with her to Cannon Beach, Oregon for three days. It was the first week of December and the weather was mild in this charming town where we enjoyed walks on long sandy beaches, appealing shops and great restaurants. We hoped to do some Christmas shopping.

When I arrived home after only two days, Peter met me at the door. Looking into his flushed face, I saw immediately that something was terribly wrong. I felt his forehead. Hot. I took his temperature. One hundred two. I had no sooner convinced him that he must go to bed than he began to cough up blood. Terrified, I said I would call the doctor.

"No. We are not going to bother Dr. Yee. It's just a sore throat. I'll be fine in the morning."

Neither of us slept that night. Tylenol and cool cloths did not bring his fever down. I wanted to call 9-1-1 but he said, "No. I am not going to have an ambulance come here and disturb the neighborhood. They'll have all their lights going. Maybe even their sirens. I don't want that."

"I can hardly be concerned about the neighborhood. You're very sick and you need medical care that I cannot give you. I can tell them not to turn on their lights and sirens," I said. "They wouldn't anyway in the middle of the night in a residential neighborhood."

"If you call them I won't go. I'm not that sick." He struggled to take a deep breath and launched into a coughing frenzy.

"Look at you. Your fever keeps inching up and I can't get it down. Even a little," I said, becoming more frantic each minute. "I'm going to call."

"No." He coughed some more. "I won't go. They can't take me if I refuse to go."

At five o'clock I called the triage line at the oncology clinic.

Dr. Yee called me back at 7:30. "I need to see him," he said. "I'll be at my office in Lakewood today. Please call there and make an appointment to bring him in."

I called the Lakewood clinic when they were open. The receptionist said to bring him at 1:30 that afternoon. Peter could not stand or walk by himself by that time. When we reached the clinic, it was necessary for me to locate a wheelchair in the hospital area to transport him from the car. The nurse later settled us in an examination room where Peter slumped forward, hardly able to sit without additional support. We waited forty-five minutes to see Dr. Yee. By this time exhausted, in near hysteria, it did not occur to me that I should call their attention to our long wait. We later learned that the receptionist had failed to tell the doctor that we had arrived.

"You say he was spitting up blood?" Dr. Yee asked me and without waiting for an answer, he added, "That's very dramatic."

"I wanted to call last night but he wouldn't allow it," I said, believing I had failed both my husband and Dr. Yee.

"He needs to go into the hospital this afternoon. I'll call and see if they have a bed." Dr. Yee left the room.

Peter turned to me and said, "I don't need to go into the hospital."

"You're very sick. You need to be where they can help you."

"I'm not sick. I'm feeling better now. I haven't coughed up blood since this morning."

. "Yes, that's good, but you need to get checked out here at the hospital." Somewhere inside me, I understood that this was an indication Peter's condition had worsened, but I was not ready to internalize that, so relieved had I been earlier when he had stopped coughing up blood.

Dr. Yee returned. "They have a bed. My nurse will tell you where to take him."

I am sure it was only minutes, but it seemed like hours passed between the time we left Dr. Yee's office and the nurses settled Peter in a hospital room. He seemed comfortable and I suggested that I would go home, clean up, and try to get some sleep.

I heard the telephone ringing as I walked into the house. It was a nurse from the hospital.

"Mrs. Dally?"

"Yes?"

"I'm calling to tell you that Dr. Yee is moving your husband to the special care unit downstairs."

"What does that mean?"

"Doctor thinks he has pneumonia. They have equipment in the special care unit to help him breathe."

"Do you think I should come back to the hospital?"

She hesitated. "I think I would if I were you."

"I'll be there in about half an hour." I hung up the phone. I called our son, John, on Vashon Island and asked him to meet me at the hospital.

I arrived there to find the entrance locked. I found my way through the maze of parking lots and buildings to the emergency entrance. Security took me directly to the special care unit. It was difficult to come to terms with the reality of Peter's condition. When a man is as robust and healthy as he has been, even though cancer has corrupted his body, an illness as swift and devastating as pneumonia, can be traumatic for those of us around him.

I stood beside Peter's bed, shocked by the change in the short time since I had left him. This is my fault, I thought. I shouldn't have left him alone for three days. I held his hand and prayed with him. Even though the doctor had started administering morphine, Peter was out of his head with pain. His heart had gone into atrial fibrillation and he had been placed on a heart monitor. Without my noticing, the pulmonary specialist arrived and attempted to extract fluid from his right lung. The doctors asked me to wait outside his room.

I telephoned Monica and Tess in Alaska and our younger son, Kurt, in Montana. I thought they should come. I would not permit myself to believe that Peter might die, but I needed them. I wanted my children with us. I could not put into words how I felt that night as I summoned them to their father's bedside. Words would have made it a crisis. Again, I thought, this is my fault.

John came on the last ferry from Vashon Island and stayed in the room with his dad through the night. Having had little rest for forty-eight hours, I tried to sleep in the waiting room. Dr. Yee woke me at 1:30 a.m.

"The pulmonologist has not been able to extract fluid from Father Peter's lung."

"I called our children in Alaska and Montana and asked them to come."

He nodded. He didn't smile.

The airport shuttle brought Tess and Monica to the hospital the next day. Being together had a calming effect on all of us. We kept our watch beside Peter's hospital bed and took turns going home to sleep a few hours at a time.

Restlessness tugged at me. At home, I wanted to be at the hospital and at the hospital I wanted to be home. I felt torn, a reluctant stranger to this prayerful vigil.

While my husband fought for every breath, I waited. The doctors attempted to drain his lung a second time. I wondered if the fluid was rising still more and he was slowly drowning in spite of their efforts. However, I was afraid to ask this question, for I did not want to know the answer. After several days—I don't know how many—Peter was moved from the special care unit to the second floor and we were hopeful that his condition was improving. The first night the nurse called, concerned that he was hallucinating.

"It's the drugs, Mom," Tess said. "I'll go back to the hospital and stay with him."

With Tess in a chair beside him, Peter slept peacefully through the night.

On Sunday, the doctor tried to drain his right lung again. This time he had some success.

Bit by bit the pain eased. The distressing hallucinations became less frequent. I hoped it meant that the worst was behind us.

Time passed in a blur, caving in on itself and hardly existing in any discernable way. Visitors came and went. All prayed with Peter. A friend, Pat Norton, brought holy oil provided by Father Joseph from the tomb of St. Nicholas. Then the children were gone, back to their homes and jobs. I was alone. I could not recall ever before experiencing such tomb-like quiet in our house, empty and lifeless. I dreaded going there at night.

Each day Peter seemed stronger and more alert, his breathing less labored. After twelve days, Dr. Yee released him. Sister Irene went with me to the hospital and helped get him settled when we arrived home. Our friends from St. George Church had brought food so that I could give my full attention to Peter.

Victory, I thought. We will be home together. Peter will go out to fill the bird feeders in our back yard. He will write icons.

We will do the things we enjoy. Life will be normal again, whatever that might mean for us now.

Then the shock set in. He remained unable to stand or walk by himself. He needed a walker and constant care and attention. I could not leave him alone.

We no longer laughed.

"Who did you say is coming? I don't want to see anyone," he said each time friends called.

I encouraged them to come and stay only a few minutes, feeling that Peter needed the diversion.

It seemed that I had fallen asleep and awakened in another woman's life.

For months before the bout with pneumonia, we had talked about getting a dog. However, Peter was reluctant and we could not agree on the breed or the right time for us.

I relaxed with a cup of fresh coffee beside Peter in our living room. He was getting stronger and it seemed a good time to talk about a dog.

"I loved Kaylo," I said. Kaylo, a standard poodle, had belonged to our grandchildren.

"Are you crazy? She weighed more than a hundred pounds."

Not a good beginning, I thought. "I know she was big, but she had a lovely disposition. They're not always that big. We could get a small standard poodle—maybe 30 to 35 pounds."

"How should I know how many sizes they come in?" Peter turned away, annoyed and disgusted at my suggestion to consider a standard poodle, or—I realized—any dog at all.

"I know we haven't had a dog since we lived on Vashon Island, but maybe it's time to think about a pet again."

"It would be a lot of responsibility. In addition, it would take a lot of care. There would be training. What about the expense?"

"Maybe we could get a miniature poodle." I smiled, hoping to get him interested.

"You sound like it's settled."

"No..."

"You'll do what you want to do anyway." He turned back to his book.

We had not owned a pet for twenty-three years. It would be a big change for us, like starting a second family. Still, it seemed right to me that we should get a dog. I could not explain my rationale. It just seemed right. I knew we had to do something to take our minds off Peter's illness and the progressively poor health that now seemed inevitable. I just did not want to come home alone to an empty lifeless house again.

As a devoted reader of the classified section of the newspaper, I had repeatedly seen an ad for standard poodles. I called the kennel in Chehalis, thirty miles from our home. "We're older people and my husband is ill. Our son had a poodle that weighed more than a hundred pounds. We can't handle a dog that big. It would have to be much smaller, about the size of a large miniature."

"I have two black females that might be suitable," the owner said.

"What will they weigh?"

"Both of these will be small standards, thirty-five to forty pounds."

"Let me talk to my husband and I'll call you back."

"Would you like to see them and their parents? They are all on site and should be the same size as the parents when they are grown."

"I'll have to call you back."

Peter agreed to let me look at the puppies and think about buying one. In my heart, I knew there was a puppy out there for us, maybe not one of these, but one somewhere. Already I had chosen a name for her.

John took me to Chehalis and we came home with Josephine, ten weeks old and a trembling ball of soft black hair. Even I was surprised to find myself the owner of this new puppy. Moreover, I was unprepared. I did not have a place for her to sleep that night and I sure didn't know how I would introduce her to Peter. She was not exactly a surprise. However, well, she would surprise him.

We had barely gotten into the house when I put Josephine down and she peed on the kitchen floor.

I slipped in it and fell.

This caused more trembling on Josephine's part and tears from me.

Peter reproached me from his recliner. "I thought you were just going to look at the dogs. I knew you would do this. Now you've fallen. Are you all right?"

"I'm okay. I'll be fine."

"We have no business with a dog. You'll have to take it back tomorrow."

Later when I limped into the bedroom, I did not admit to him how badly my ankle throbbed. Josephine snuggled next to me in bed and slept soundly next to my heart.

Already I had fallen in love with her, but Peter had definitely placed this little black intruder on strict probation. The next day, I made an appointment with the doctor. I learned that I had fractured my ankle and would need to wear an orthopedic boot for six weeks—In actuality it stretched into nine.

Now we were two semi-invalids living alone with a new baby. Peter grumbled when she wandered from the kitchen or missed the newspaper on the floor when she peed. Still, he grudgingly held her on his lap when he could not avoid my insistence. "Well, she does give us something else to think about," he conceded.

I smiled.

Christmas was days away and this year it was our turn to have John, Sherry and the children at our house. I was not at all sure I could do it with a broken ankle. Then I decided that I had to try. This last episode with pneumonia had demonstrated to us how fragile life is and particularly so for Peter, a man who had been living with multiple myeloma for more than six years. We knew that the disease had compromised his immune system, and now we understood the perils we could face because of that. I wanted to make this Christmas special for him and the family. Our daughters would not be able to come again so soon, but John and his family would be here and possibly Kurt who lived in

Montana. The children said they would help me and we agreed to go ahead with our plans to have Christmas at our house.

The day arrived and Peter was able to sit to celebrate Mass for the family. Paul served the altar and Caitlin read the epistle. It was a special moment for all of us, but I think especially for me. Our family gathered around a table is the heart of our relationship as parents and children. Throughout our lives, through stresses, childhood illness, accidents, and financial difficulties, mealtime brought us together and restored balance and wholeness to our lives. It didn't matter what we had to eat, prime rib or tuna gravy on biscuits, or if there were candles and flowers on the table. The important thing was the family sharing it together.

That January the snow came and we could not leave our house for two weeks. The time was a welcome reprieve from the continual succession of medical appointments we had endured two to three times a week since Peter's pneumonia. By this time, he had advanced from the walker to a cane, and he stubbornly asserted that he needed it only to steady himself. I could not help but admire his unbroken spirit when he crossed the back yard each day to fill the bird feeders, taking with him Josephine, who by now was simply "Josie".

On one of these mornings, I watched him hobble across the yard, praying that he would not slip and fall. Josie followed him. The snow was deep and her belly dragged across the top as she timidly tried to place her small paws in his footprints. When they reached the bird feeder, Peter looked down at her and I could see him talking. She watched as he opened the feeder and laid it down on the snow. She leaned over, sniffed, and inspected it. He talked to her and she looked up at him. It was a touching scene: this man who had not wanted this puppy, and this baby poodle, innocent and trusting. Soon they finished and Josie followed him back to the house. I felt sure she would find her way into his heart.

Exhausted from this short walk, Peter dropped back into his blue leather recliner by the fireplace. He pulled the patchwork lap robe—made for him by Merylin Young in Tulsa—up to his chin. His head bent forward, his priest's office book lay open in his lap. He had been up for only a short time, but already he had fallen asleep.

Outside, the sky was a clear blue, free of clouds after the sprinkling of new snow during the night. The winter sun streamed in the window from the east and made a rosy halo on Mt. Rainier in the distance. As I watched him, I thought of how a bout with pneumonia only weeks earlier had left this strong man weak and exhausted.

Now his talk frequently centered on the question of why he had not died. "There must be something more God wants me to do," he said repeatedly.

"Haven't you done enough?" I laughed, chiding him for his energetic ministry of fifty-four years. "I mean, you've given your entire life to God. Can't you rest now, knowing that you've done all you have been called to do?"

"I don't know, Mary. I don't know. When I look back, there are so many things I should have done differently. Ways I failed my congregations. Ways I failed God. And you." He turned to me, his eyes filled with pain and sadness.

Then I would try to convince him to use this present time for us. He had dedicated himself wholly to God's work and now he could rest in His peace. I reminded him that this was our quiet time to recollect and draw strength from our love for each other, the exciting life we had shared, and all that surely must lie ahead for us, as eventually one must face going on without the other.

I watched him sleep.

-37-

Idealists that we are, we expected life to return to normal. However, Peter no sooner recovered from the pneumonia than he contracted a bacterial infection through a tiny scratch on his leg. This required daily antibiotic infusions for more than a week at St. Joseph Hospital in Tacoma.

Shocked by this new vulnerability, I wondered if he would regain his former state of health. His immune system was clearly at its lowest.

In May 2004, less than five months later, he developed strep pneumonia. We caught it earlier this time and it was not so serious. However, he was hospitalized for another six days during which time the doctor diagnosed him with diabetes.

"You can thank us for the diabetes. We did that to you," Dr. Yee said, the irony being that in order to help him, the cancer drug's side effects had impaired Peter's health in another way.

Now we would add to our schedule diabetes classes, twice-daily blood sugar checks, and still more medical specialists to see regularly. I wondered if we would ever regain some sense of normalcy.

Two weeks later Dr. Yee told us that the blood protein marker for multiple myeloma had become a concern. To stave off the disease's progress he added daily doses of thalidomide to the steroid treatment. It was not until after Peter's diagnosis seven years earlier, that thalidomide, the drug that had caused birth defects in the 1960s, became known as an effective treatment in the control of multiple myeloma. Cancer treatment requires large doses of thalidomide and, again, I wondered about the side effects.

Dr. Yee ordered immunoglobulin infusions (IVIG) at twenty-eight day intervals to stave off the growth of myeloma tumors in Peter's bone marrow and boost his immune system—this, in addition to the steroid treatment, thalidomide, and zomata for bone strength. We hoped that this means of managing his disease would slow or stop the growth of myeloma tumors. Ours was a perilous journey, a delicate balance between toxic substances and their positive effect on the cancer.

Peter's hopeful outlook was the light on our horizon as we again placed his future in the hands of medical experts. His belief that the Holy Father's prayers and the prayers of our family and friends had sustained him, and would continue to see him through each crisis, was simple and straightforward. In addition, I felt sure that a lifetime of physical exercise and good nutrition had prepared him for the past challenges and those we would face in the future. Peter's good attitude made my job as his caregiver and chief support immeasurably easier. However, realistically, I was afraid. For seven years, this disease had ravaged his body. I had witnessed the gradual decline. I could not look to the future with any hope or expectation of recovering the level of health he enjoyed before the pneumonia. His decline was inevitable.

In January 2006, Peter had his monthly cancer clinic appointment. We stood in Dr. Yee's office and talked for a few minutes when Peter suddenly crumpled to the floor. His body simply and gently collapsed mid-sentence. It did not seem real. I stood by, shocked and helpless. Hearing the nurse call for oxygen and emergency medical personnel brought some sense of reality back to me.

Moments earlier Peter had been engaged in a lively discussion with Dr. Yee and now he appeared lifeless on the floor. The nurse indicated I should wait in the hall, allowing space in the small treatment room for the nursing staff. Muffled voices came to me from inside the room. Dr. Yee waited beside me. We watched.

"What caused this? Could it be that the nurse administered the IVIG too fast?" I asked, thinking that there must be a particular protocol for this infusion.

Dr. Yee looked surprised. "No, I don't think so." However, he turned and went down the hall in the direction of the infusion clinic.

It was not until the EMTs wheeled Peter out on the gurney that I knew he was still breathing. Then in the hall, I felt an EMT take my arm and guide me to the ambulance.

In the emergency room, we waited. Staff came and checked his heart rate again and again. They assured me that a hospital room would be available soon.

I called John, and moments later Paul and Caitlin arrived from their school. John would come from Vashon Island on the next ferry. Deacon Joseph Wargacki came from his job on the oncology floor. He assured me everything he needed would be done for Peter. We waited. It was not until evening, six hours after he collapsed, that the hospital room was ready.

Days later, the doctors determined that the prolonged thalidomide treatment had caused his heart rate to drop suddenly. I recalled the several momentary blackouts I had witnessed and the fact that Peter had stopped driving several months earlier. However, no other collapse had been as dramatic as this one. A few days later, the cardiologist implanted a pacemaker as a preventative measure. This meant still another medical specialist to see regularly.

Nevertheless, Peter continued to have cardiac problems.

Add to this, the other side affects of severe neuropathy, fluid retention, inability to focus, difficulty walking. Peter had two cataract surgeries, the second one having complications that required an emergency trip to Swedish Hospital in Seattle where doctors performed three additional surgeries the same day to save his vision.

The frequent medical crises and the constant stream of exhausting doctor's appointments had become our life. Peter was too exhausted to do anything else. When he had an appointment, we tried to schedule it so that we could enjoy lunch in a restaurant, but sometimes exhaustion pre-empted even this. His illness was all consuming, both for him and for me.

Still, through these distressing episodes and ongoing trials, we felt grateful for his quality of life. We knew of other multiple myeloma patients who could not tolerate the steroid and thalidomide regimen. Considering that, Peter held up relatively well.

He found ways to stay productive. He continued his daily study of the scriptures and the Greek and Hebrew translations he worked on each morning. He unswervingly prayed his morning, noon and evening offices, and the intercessory prayers that had always been so important to him. Although he was not able to attend any of the daily liturgies, he assisted at St. George Church almost every Sunday. We took short walks in the neighborhood with Josie, resting on a garden wall, midway. He never missed Book Notes on C-Span and he read every one of the abundant American history books that had flooded the bookstores after the 9-11 attack. He told his favorite stories—old jokes and life experiences—to anyone who would listen. He and Josie, our now-adult poodle, fed the birds every morning and evening, after which she lay down beside his chair and they both napped. He talked of finishing several icons and the painting he had begun for Paul, our grandson.

After he got the pacemaker, Peter stopped celebrating the Divine Liturgy for the Sisters at Holy Theophany Monastery. The Sisters had become an important part of our life and it was difficult for him to tell them he could no longer do it. He told Father Lee Perry at St. George Church that he could only substitute for him in an emergency. To me, he said that his difficulty walking and his occasional mental confusion made it impossible to perform these duties, as he would wish.

Through all of this, Peter's appearance was remarkable. He did not lose weight. His complexion was good. His hair was only slightly thinning due to the chemicals. In short, he looked so healthy that it was difficult for people to understand how sick he was. He protested that he could not handle the numerous invitations to participate in church services and activities and I became the buffer, insisting that he was not well enough, as much as both he and I would have enjoyed the involvement.

In late 2006, ten months after he collapsed in Dr. Yee's office, Peter began to suffer the indignity of incontinence. While he was sure that the medication the urologist had prescribed was not helping the problem, he had no other symptoms to indicate a more serious condition. It was not until months later that the doctor performed an exploratory exam to determine whether there was a growth in Peter's bladder.

And yes, there was something that needed further investigation.

"This is a simple matter," the doctor said. "But, we'll need to do it at the hospital."

On April 10, 2007, as Peter lay in the hospital preparing for the procedure, we talked to his urologist.

"Will you be able to tell whether it is cancer by looking at it?" I asked.

"You don't want me to be able to tell. If I can see it with the naked eye, it's bad." His face was grave.

I was stunned. While this was yet another crisis in our long journey, we had expected that like the others before it, we could live with it. Life would go on. Now I wondered if the multiple myeloma had spread to his bladder. On the other hand it could be another cancer altogether. Again, instinctively I had felt all along that this was bad, even though the doctor repeatedly assured us that it was a simple routine matter.

The nurse took Peter into surgery and I went to the waiting area alone. I had a book to read, but the words on the page were meaningless. What if this *is* more cancer, I thought.

I recalled Dr. Browning's words in Tulsa when he diagnosed Peter: "Myeloma is a terrible disease."

I prayed that we could find still more strength. I had asked for it so many times in the past ten years and somehow, I felt that it had been granted us.

I went to the cafeteria for coffee. Returned to the waiting area and tried, without success, to read again. I watched people. Listened to other families seated in the waiting area. Their conversations avoided the real issues, the reasons for their gathering. I wanted someone to talk with, to share this impending crisis. I felt more alone than ever. We had told John not to come because of the routine nature of this procedure.

Routine? Not really, I thought. The minutes dragged.

I closed my eyes and prayed again that the tumor would not be cancer. The final prognosis by the Tulsa oncologist had been six to ten years survival and it would be ten years in May. I did not like prognoses. Still, I had to admit, ten years felt like a victory of sorts. One of the nurses in the oncology clinic had recently told us that Peter had survived using thalidomide therapy longer than any other patient they had treated. Surely, this was a testimony to prayer, his lifelong good health, and positive outlook.

This morning, though, it seemed to me that we were at a turning point in this disease. In my heart, I knew that the growth was not "nothing". There were just too many signs. The incontinence. The distended abdomen. The fluid retention so extreme in one leg and absent in the other. While we had repeatedly asked every doctor about this, we had never received a reasonable response. All these signs. These warnings. Now, the waiting.

Finally, I saw Peter's urologist come into the area. He looked around the room. I rose and waved.

I read the outcome in his expression.

"No," I said.

"I'm afraid it's bad. There is no doubt that it is malignant. I could not remove the tumor; it has gone through the muscle wall."

"Through the muscle. Does that mean it has spread?" I felt numb.

"It is my opinion that it has. His kidneys are swollen and at risk. He will need to have his bladder removed. The University of Washington does that surgery."

I remembered that multiple myeloma could involve the kidneys, leaving them compromised. Possibly the elevated protein, I thought. Sometimes the patient goes into kidney failure and that becomes the actual cause of death. In a split second my mind raced, looking for some logic, some pattern.

Numbed by his words, I asked, "Where do we go?"

"You will need to go to the University of Washington Urology Clinic in Seattle."

"Do you think we got it in time?"

"I don't know. Time is everything now and I promise I will get you into the university doctors as soon as possible. The sooner they see him, the better." As he rose to leave, he turned to me. "Mary, you need to have your children with you when he has the surgery." I felt stunned. Did this mean the doctor thinks he could die in the operating room, I wondered.

"Three of them live at some distance," I heard myself say.

Yes, I needed to think about the children, I thought.

"You can go in to see him in a few minutes. They'll come and get you."

"Does he know?" I choked back tears.

"I'll come in to talk to you both in a little while."

As I waited, I could not take it all in. It seemed unreal. Surely, this was happening to another person. Not me. Not after everything we have been through.

Still, it has been ten years. Did I really think we could go on like this indefinitely?

At the University of Washington Urology Clinic Peter underwent a thorough exam. The doctors were certain that the cancer had not gone through the muscle wall.

That was the good news.

However, they emphasized that time was of the essence and, while their next opening for surgery was eight weeks away, they said they would do everything they could to get Peter an earlier date.

In the meantime, Peter's condition worsened. Though I was not a medical professional, it seemed to me that his kidneys were beginning to shut down. I could find no other explanation. He had little control, if any, and his output was minimal. He complained of back pain.

It was not like him to complain.

Peter attempted to continue his scripture study, meditation, and prayer, but I noticed that he would begin, and within minutes, his bible and prayer book were lying in his lap and he was asleep. He rarely went to his study to work on Greek and Hebrew translations. When he did, I would find him bent over his desk, pen in hand, unable to focus on things that, until recently, were routine.

Denying what I knew in my heart to be inevitable, that the cancer was inoperable, I could not sit and do nothing. I emailed our family, friends, and former parishioners, asking them to pray for Peter, and to pray for an earlier surgery date. I received responses and assurances of prayer from people of all faiths. We felt blessed, and relieved, when ten days after the doctor's examination, his assistant called to say they had a surgery date scheduled later that week.

Our daughters in Hawaii and Alaska and our son in Montana had flight reservations for the original date of surgery. The doctors seemed so certain that the cancer was contained in the bladder that the children decided they would not come for the surgery. Instead, they would come to be with their dad while he recovered. This decision was a difficult one for them as well as for us, but it seemed the right one under the circumstances.

The morning Peter went into surgery, a CT scan further confirmed the doctor's conviction that the cancer had not spread outside the bladder. This latest confirmation of the earlier diagnosis had given Peter the confidence to believe that, while he would have to live with the inconvenience of a urostomy, he would survive yet another medical crisis.

We hoped for the best outcome.

Our son John, from Vashon Island waited with me in the family area. Our doctor expected the surgery to take about six hours. He said someone would come to give us a progress report about halfway through.

When I saw the surgeon approaching our table after only two hours, I felt relieved. Surely, this would be good news.

He sat down at our table and looked from me to John. "The bladder is full of cancer and it has spread through the muscle wall. If I try to remove it, Father Dally could bleed to death on the operating table. His kidneys are inflamed and swollen and I believe urine is backing up into them. It will not be very long before they begin to shutdown. There is only a trickle of urine passing through his bladder now. I suggest that we make him more comfortable by taking a section of his colon to create a conduit from his kidneys to an opening in his side so that he can pass urine and his kidneys can regain their health. He may wish to have chemotherapy or radiation. You will need to see his oncologist to determine that."

They make it sound so black and white, I thought, so clinical. They offer hope and then nothing. I wanted to tell them that I knew in my heart that they were wrong all along, that the cancer had spread. He is strong. Still, how long can this go on?

Finally, I asked, "Will further treatment cure the bladder cancer?"

"In these cases there is the possibility that a combination of chemo and radiation will shrink the tumor enough that it could be surgically removed."

Still, so clinical.

"Well, let's by all means make him more comfortable with the procedure you suggested," John said.

"Yes," I said, numbed by visions of the uncertainties and challenges of the days ahead.

"We'll go ahead with it then. He is doing well otherwise. He should have a full recovery from the surgery. We will be finished in, perhaps, another two hours. I'll be out to talk to you when it's over."

-38-

How can I explain the well-meant siege of "medical treatment by committee" that is inherent in a large teaching hospital?

Each of the "-ologists" came and poked and prodded and questioned and ran still more tests. We tried to be patient and realize that these interns and residents were doctors-in-training who worked under the watchful guidance of medical experts. All the while, all that Peter really wanted was to go home.

I received detailed instructions from the urostomy nurse on how to care for Peter. In near panic, I tried to convince myself that I could do this, that I could care for his intimate physical needs. It would take a new kind of courage for both of us and I prayed that God would grant it.

Social services people came. The end-of-life doctor, a young woman who could not possibly know the impact of her message, as she seemed reluctant to deliver it with the depth that was called for. In a contradiction, another resident arrived to talk about home health care and wellness. We were told the urologists recommended chemotherapy and radiation to shrink the tumor. Still more bewildering was the social worker who said that our oncologist, Dr. Yee, recommended hospice care.

We were overwhelmed and confused as medical professionals streamed into Peter's hospital room, made recommendations and just as abruptly, withdrew them. I felt jerked around and dehumanized as they reduced the thread of my husband's life to disagreements, contradictions, and ultimately, medical technology.

Somehow, this surgery had felt like an experiment from the beginning.

John came from Vashon Island every day. Monica and Tess arrived from Hawaii and Alaska. Peter's sister, Sister Elsbeth flew in from Jerusalem. The family, all but Kurt—he would come later from Montana—was together.

In the hospital cafeteria, we talked, bewildered by the conflicting messages we were getting. "Don't they realize that Dad has been dealing with life and death issues for the more than fifty years of his ministry? They need to be real with him," Tess said.

"One doctor says one thing and another comes in and says something else. I don't understand what's going on." Monica said.

"I don't think they have taken time to know him. To ask him what it is that he wants," I said.

Several days later, we took Peter home from the hospital. I had requested home-care equipment through the hospital social worker but none had been delivered. Even with the support we had presumably been given, and because the varying opinions of the University doctors contradicted Dr. Yee's recommendations,

I had no idea where to turn for help. After one night at home, I knew I could not care for Peter without a hospital bed. I found the home care number the University Hospital had given me and called them. The bed and other needed equipment arrived within an hour even though the day was Sunday. On Monday, the home care nurse came and we continued the discussion of what appropriate care for Peter should be.

"Are you doing home care or hospice?" Reta asked as the family sat with her around Peter's bed. Her direct question demonstrated sensitivity and gave a pivotal point at which to begin a plan.

"It's unclear what is needed," I said.

She explained the advantage and intricacies of each. "Home care is limited. Hospice provides everything that you will need. Most especially, care to the end of life. Father Peter could go from home care to hospice easily. However, the reverse is complicated." Reta looked around the room. Peter lay quietly in his hospital bed.

More perplexed than ever, the children and I looked at each other. None of us had an answer.

"Who is your oncologist?" she asked.

"Dr. Lorrin Yee," I answered. "At St. Joseph Hospital in Tacoma." I took a deep breath. "His orders are for hospice, but the University doctors are ordering home care. Dr. Yee does not advise chemo or radiation."

"What do the University doctors say?" Reta asked.

"That Dr. Yee would determine whether he should have treatment." I hesitated. "But, they are also going beyond that and telling us Peter will get well. It's very confusing."

"I'll call Dr. Yee," Reta said.

I felt relieved that someone had taken decisive action to help us deal with the confusion between the various physicians' advice and our desire to care for Peter in the best possible way. I got Dr. Yee on the phone and Reta talked to him for several minutes. From her responses, I was certain he was saying the same things to her that he had told us. I also began to realize that Dr. Yee's recommendation was the correct one. However, I did not have the courage to request hospice. Peter was alert and he needed to make that decision himself.

Reta handed the phone to Peter. "Father, he wants to talk to you."

With my heart in my throat and tears in my eyes, I watched and listened while Dr. Yee talked to Peter. John touched his dad's shoulder. Monica and Tess moved close to stand beside me. Peter handed the phone back to Reta and turned to me. "He recommends hospice," he said. I grasped my husband's hand and held it to my face. I stroked his forehead and kissed him.

"I don't want to leave you," he whispered.

"But you'll always be with me, Love. We are now all that we have been to each other and I will carry that with me always."

Although Peter had seemed to accept that his time was limited, he maintained his wholesome attitude and continued to try to regain his strength. The patient coordinator in the surgeon's office at the University called to say that the doctor wanted Peter to come for a follow-up appointment.

I replied, "I think the sixty mile trip would be too strenuous for him. He is receiving hospice care. His energy is limited and I can't see putting him through the long drive to Seattle."

A few minutes later, the assistant called me back to say that the doctor said it was very important for him to see Peter.

We drove to Seattle for the appointment and again, the physicians insisted that Peter could get well.

What was the point of this?

It had given Peter false hope. Still more uncertainty. More stress. It had accomplished nothing.

Then Dr. Yee's nurse called and said that he would like to see Peter. As I look back now, I wonder if this was the result of the University doctor's latest assessment. I do not know. However, again, it felt like a kind of victimization.

"These trips are very hard on him," I said to the nurse. "Is it really necessary or just another exercise in futility?"

"Dr. Yee would very much like to see how Father is doing and determine if he can do anything to make him more comfortable."

I turned to Peter and told him what the nurse said.

He nodded.

"Well, all right," I said to the nurse.

This made some sense to me.

The appointment with Dr. Yee took place three weeks after the failed surgery to remove the cancer from Peter's bladder. We had been going to the oncology clinic at St. Joseph Hospital every four weeks for almost six years for his regular consultations, zomata infusions, and IV-IG transfusions. The office staff had been like family, greeting us with smiles, and joking with Peter. We had appreciated—and come to expect—not only their good care, but also their emotional support. We never felt that they viewed Peter as just another disease to treat. They had always been wonderful.

However, on this visit, things changed. No one seemed to know us. The receptionist even asked Peter for his name. When we encountered the nurses, we knew so well, they seemed not to see us. Only one of the staff acknowledged us. She hugged Peter and said that she was sorry to hear the news and that she would be praying for us.

What was wrong, I wondered. Now, when we needed their support and encouragement more than ever, they had withdrawn. Surely, they had not meant to react to us this way. I felt I must have misunderstood. Still, it was clear. Each person had pulled back and let go of us. Why? Sadly, Peter felt it too. Later, as the days passed, I tried to forget it, but it stayed with me for months. Even today, I feel the sadness of it, especially for Peter.

When we saw Dr. Yee, he asked Peter some questions and then he placed his hand on Peter's arm when he said, "I wish I had a better prognosis. If there is anything you need, Father, have Mary call me."

Peter smiled. "I want to thank you for the good care you have given me, Dr. Yee. I know that because of you I have had ten pretty amazing years in spite of this disease."

That was the last time we saw Dr. Yee.

I can only say that the weeks that followed were filled with immense joy. It is a great privilege to care for a loved one at the end. As Peter waited to be taken into the loving arms of God, we experienced clarity and deep gratitude for a life well lived.

There were no long talks about the meaning of life, no startling theological revelations. His joy in having our children around him was evident in his face, far greater than words could express. I sat by his bed and at night I slept in the bed near him and I wondered, what will I do when he is gone.

We prayed together.

Each morning and evening, he asked for his Bible, office book, and intercession book, determined to continue his habit of prayer. Yet they only lay beside him on the bed, unopened.

Bishop William Skurla, of the Byzantine Eparchy of Van Nuys whom Peter served while assisting at St. George Byzantine Catholic Church, wrote a comforting letter and sent him a beautiful bedside icon.

Bishop John Michael, Romanian Catholic bishop to the Sisters at Holy Theophany Monastery, brought Holy Communion and anointed Peter with holy oil. He took Peter's hand and said, "Father Peter, I want to thank you for taking care of my Sisters when they had no one else to come to them."

Peter had served the Sisters even though they were out of favor with the Byzantine eparchy at the time, jeopardizing his own standing as a priest with Byzantine faculties. Tears rolled down my cheeks as I thought of my husband's many instances of courage and integrity of purpose, those times when he acted against the advice of associates because he knew it was the right thing to do.

Others came to see him, to pray with him. I did not turn them away, asking them to stay only a few minutes.

In the last days, he no longer spoke or responded to our voices. Still, when I prayed the Lord's Prayer with him, his lips moved with the words. The children sang some of his favorite songs and we saw his toes move, as he attempted to keep the rhythm.

The last day, the children and I never left Peter's bedside. We held him and prayed with him.

Peter fell asleep in the Lord on July 6, 2007. Three weeks earlier, we had celebrated our fiftieth wedding anniversary.

GLOSSARY

Apostolic Succession   The sequence of apostolic succession in ordained ministry begins with the apostles themselves and continues down through to the bishops of the present time. This is marked by lawful, valid ordination conferred on bishops of the church.

Benedictine   Followers of the rule established by St. Benedict shortly before his death in 543 AD.

Benedictine Oblate   Men and women who associate themselves with a Benedictine monastic community in order to strengthen and enrich their Christian way of life.

Biretta   A square cap with three or four ridges or peaks, sometimes surmounted by a tuft, traditionally worn by Roman Catholic clergy and some Anglican and Episcopal priests.

Bishop Eusebius J. Beltran   Bishop of Tulsa, Oklahoma from 1978-1992. Pope John Paul II appointed him Archbishop of Oklahoma City November 24, 1992. Now serves as Archbishop Emeritus of the Archdiocese of Oklahoma City.

Book of Common Prayer   Refers to the 1928 edition authorized for use in the Episcopal Church prior to 1979. The Book of Common Prayer is the primary book of public worship, ritual, and prayers used by those Christians – Episcopalians and Anglicans – who look to the Church of England for their roots. (See Great Schism of 1054.)

Capuchin   An order of Franciscan Friars Minor.

Cardinal Bernard Law   Bishop of Springfield-Cape Gerardeau, Missouri from 1973-84. He was appointed the Vatican Liaison for the Pastoral Provision in the U.S. by Pope John Paul II from 1981-2003. Archbishop of Boston 1984-2002. Named to College of Cardinals in 1985. After resigning as Archbishop of Boston he was appointed to several authoritative positions in Rome and the Vatican by the Holy Father. He is currently archpriest at the Basilica di Santa Maria Maggiore in Rome.

Catechism of the Catholic Church   The text that is a summary of Catholic doctrine.

<u>Catechize</u> To instruct someone in the ways of the Christian faith, especially by means of the Catechism of the Catholic Church.

<u>Catholic Extension Society, USA</u>   Founded by Bishop Francis Kelley in 1905 to promote the mission of the Catholic Church in rural and mission areas of the United States.

<u>Catholic Heritage</u>   Many Episcopal priests aligned with the Oxford Movement in 19th Century England whereby it was believed that only one Church could claim historic Catholicity and the Church of England (Episcopal) should necessarily be a part of that historic Church. That the Roman Catholic, Orthodox and Episcopalians were "separated brethren", branches of the same vine and that as an accident of secular history, Episcopalians were not longer under the Holy Father. (Source: Rev. Jack D. Barker, 1993)

<u>Charismatic</u>   The word comes from the Greek and means in a broad sense any favor or gift. In the technical sense as used by St. Paul and applied by Christians, it means those extraordinary gifts granted to early Christian communities for the benefit of others and for the spread of Christianity.

<u>Decretal</u>   A decision handed down by the Pope, generally on questions of discipline (as in an exception to priestly celibacy) usually in the form of a letter.

<u>Divine Liturgy</u>   The Eucharistic Rite of the Eastern Catholic Church, based on the liturgies of St. Basil the Great and St. John Chrysostom.

<u>Dorothy Day</u>   1897-1980 – An American journalist who became a social activist and devout Catholic. Known for her social justice campaigns in defense of the poor, forsaken, hungry and homeless. With Peter Maurin, she founded the Catholic Worker Movement in 1933, espousing nonviolence, and hospitality for the impoverished and downtrodden.

<u>Ecumenical</u>   The movement towards co-operation among Christians.

<u>Eastern Rite Catholics</u>   In union with the Pope, eastern rite Catholics most often have their origins in Eastern Europe. Located geographically in close proximity to the Ottoman Empire, which lasted from the 13th century until the end of World War I, the countries of Eastern Europe are significantly influenced by the people of Greece and Turkey. The Byzantine rite, also known as Ruthenian Rite originated in Slavic countries. Maronites and Melkites originate in Lebanon. Tridentine refers to the traditional form of the Latin Mass. There are more than twenty different rites within the Roman Catholic Church.

<u>Eparchy</u>   The diocese of an eastern Catholic church. As in Holy Protection of Mary Byzantine Catholic Eparchy of Phoenix (formerly the Byzantine Eparchy of Van Nuys).

<u>Faculties</u>   Authorization granted to a priest by the bishop of a Catholic diocese or eparchy to perform the sacraments.

<u>Filioque</u>   This Latin word, translated "from the Son" is used in the Nicene Creed to declare the twofold procession of God the Holy Spirit from the "Father and from the Son."   It was first added to the Nicene Creed at the Council of Toledo, A.D. 589.

<u>Fraidy Hole</u>   Slang term for a tornado shelter.

<u>Franciscan</u>   Members of the Order of Friars Minor that was founded by St. Francis of Assisi in 1209.

<u>General Convention of the Protestant Episcopal Church 1976</u>   The governing body that made irreversible changes to the doctrine, discipline, and worship of the Episcopal Church. The objection by priests and laymen dedicated to the church's Catholic heritage was based on a lack of proper authority and that such moves would set back hopes for reunion with Rome and Orthodox Christians indefinitely. Prayer book revisions were seen as diluting its doctrinal base and the ordination of women was seen as unacceptable to either the Roman Catholic or Orthodox Churches and, therefore would risk setting back ecumenical relations for years. It was perceived that a Catholicism without Rome and opposed to Rome required too great a compromise of conscience; it was also thought that the new openness and renewal in the Roman Catholic Church since the Second Vatican Council eliminated many of the previously held concerns of catholic minded Episcopalians. For many it seemed that

continued separation could not be tolerated. (Source: Rev. Jack D. Barker, 1993)

<u>Gnosticism</u> A blanket term for various religions and sects most prominent in the first few centuries A.D. Its name comes from the Greek word for knowledge, *gnosis*, referring to the idea that there is special, hidden knowledge that only a few may possess. Often associated with occult teachings.

<u>Great Schism of 1054</u> Divided Christianity into Western Catholicism and Eastern Orthodoxy. Though dated 1054, the East-West Schism was actually the result of an extended period of estrangement between the two church bodies. The primary causes of the Schism were disputes over papal authority. The Pope claimed he held authority over the four Eastern patriarchs while Eastern Orthodoxy claimed that the primacy of the Patriarch of Rome was only honorary and thus he had authority only over Western Christians, and over the insertion of the filioque clause into the Nicene Creed. These were the major disputes, but there were other, catalysts for the schism, including variance over liturgical practices and conflicting claims of jurisdiction. The Church split along doctrinal, theological, linguistic, political, and geographic lines, and the fundamental breach has never been healed. For the most part the Western and the Eastern Churches are separate. Each takes the view that it is the "One Holy Catholic and Apostolic Church", implying that the other group left the true church during the Schism.

<u>Healing Mass</u> A Mass at which special prayers for physical and spiritual healing are central, and often includes the laying on of hands and other expressions of praise.

<u>Heretical</u> To be outside the accepted truths revealed by God or proposed for belief by the Catholic Church.

<u>High Churchmen</u> Episcopal priests and lay persons, who being faithful to the historic Catholic thought and practice in Anglicanism, adhered to a "higher" form of worship that was more Catholic in faith and practice. Faithful to the concept of a Roman Catholic heritage.

<u>Holy Father</u> This title of reverence is accorded the pope as spiritual father of the universal Church.

<u>Holy Oil</u> Sacramentals blessed by the bishop each Holy Thursday in the cathedral of the diocese. Holy oil may also come from a shrine and be the source of healing and other miracles.

<u>Holy Spirit</u> In Christianity, the third person of the Holy Trinity.

<u>Holy Theophany</u> The term, applied to the direct or hidden appearances of God in the Scriptures is derived from the Greek, meaning literally, "God in brightness." The feast day is celebrated on Epiphany, January 6th, the missionary season or showing forth.

<u>Homily</u> A more or less brief, instructive discourse on a passage of scripture, wherein the spiritual lesson of the text is made clear, especially the readings assigned to the Sundays or days of obligation. The basic form of the preaching art.

<u>Incardination</u> The formal act whereby a cleric is subordinated to a superior of a diocese, vicariate, or becomes a member of a religious community. Without incardination, one cannot be ordained.

<u>Ku-Klux-Klan</u> (KKK) This variously formed organization was begun in the post-Civil War years at Pulaski, Tennessee. It was a secret group organized against Catholics, Jews, Negroes and the foreign-born. These organizations have often used terrorism and acts of intimidation such as cross-burning to oppress these groups. The KKK remains in operation in Oklahoma and various other states.

<u>Lateran Councils of 1123 and 1129</u> At the 1123 Council Pope Calistus II decreed that clerical marriages were invalid. At the 1129 Council Pope Innocent II confirmed the previous council's decree. However, priests and even popes continued to marry and have children for several hundred years after that date. The Eastern Catholic Churches outside the United States continue to this day to have married priests as an ordinary circumstance.

<u>Latin Cassock</u>   Item of clerical clothing, ankle-length robe worn by clerics in the Catholic Church and some clerics in the

Anglican, Episcopal, and Lutheran denominations. A Latin or Roman Cassock often has a series of buttons down the front while an Anglican or Episcopal cassock is usually double breasted.

Low Churchmen   This designation was given to priests and lay persons who expressed a more protestant form of worship and theology. After the 1976 General Convention of the Episcopal Church, USA, this term diminished in use.

Magisterium   The power given by Christ to the Church together with the concept of infallibility by which the Church teaches authoritatively the revealed truth of the scripture and holds forth the truth of tradition for salvation. This fact is contained in the nature and extent of the mission given to the Church and the recognized acceptance of that mission as recorded in the Acts of the Apostles.

Married priests in England – 1835   John Wordsworth, Bishop of Salisbury says that Catholic priests in England were openly married. Professor Maitland states in "Roman Catholic Law in the Church of England", that ecclesiastical law in England differed from, and was independent of, the *jus commune* (i.e. the canon law) of the Catholic Church.

Meeting in Boston, 1983   The singular gathering of Pastoral Provision priests and their wives since the program opened in 1980.

<u>Nave</u> The central part of the church, extending from the narthex to the chancel and usually flanked by aisles.

<u>Orphrey</u> The collective name given to the ornamental decoration of vestments.

<u>Orthodox Christians</u> Those under the various Orthodox jurisdictions such as Russian, Greek, Antiochian, Orthodox Church in America and others.

<u>Pastoral Provision</u> In 1980 the Holy See, in response to requests from priests and laity of the Episcopal Church who were seeking full communion with the Catholic Church, created a Pastoral Provision to provide them with special pastoral attention. The Pastoral Provision is under the jurisdiction of the Sacred Congregation for the Doctrine of the Faith whose Delegate directs the working of the Provision. It was this service rendered to the bishops of the United States by which former Episcopal priests who have been accepted as candidates for priestly ordination receive theological, spiritual, and pastoral preparation for ministry in the Catholic Church. Since 1983 more than seventy men have been ordained for priestly ministry in Catholic dioceses in the United States.

<u>Permanent Deacon</u> One who is ordained a deacon without the expectation of priesthood. Permanent deacons are often married but may not remarry if they survive a spouse. He must be willing to accept the duties of the office and the desire to remain firm in the faith.

Prioress   The superior of a religious order of women, chosen to serve for a definite period of time.

Provincial Superior   Refers to the head of the Tulsa Province of the Sisters of the Sorrowful Mother. A religious community that in the 1980s maintained eight provinces worldwide, of which three were located in the United States.

Religious   A member of a monastic order or community, especially a monk or nun.

Rite of Reconciliation   Also known as the Penance Rite or Confession of sins to God in the presence of a priest who gives the penitent counsel and absolution.

Roach   A hairstyle especially among certain Native American peoples in which the head is shaved except for a strip from front to back across the top.

Sacrament   An outward and visible sign of an inward and spiritual grace administered by someone authorized to give the sacrament with the intention of doing what the Church intends. The seven sacraments are Baptism, Holy Eucharist, penance, matrimony, anointing of the sick, confirmation, and holy orders.

Sacristy   A room in the church, usually near the altar where the sacred vessels and vestments are stored and maintained and where preparation for liturgical services is performed.

<u>Saint Augustine</u> St. Augustine is the father of Western Christianity, both Catholic and directly connected to Martin Luther and John Calvin. Oddly, his theology originates with the Gnostics, who considered the physical world bad. (Manichaeans) Most Gnostics practiced celibacy and asceticism, on the grounds that the pleasures of the flesh were evil; a few however practiced libertinism, arguing that since the body was evil they should defile it. This is where Catholicism drew its views on celibacy from, and the obsession against sex (or any pleasure at all) held by Protestants.

<u>San Damiano Crucifix</u>   The cross of St. Francis of Assisi.

<u>Skiatook</u>   William C. Rogers, last hereditary Chief of the Cherokees founded Skiatook, Oklahoma in 1872 when he established a trading post in the Cherokee Nation just to the south of Bird Creek where the stream was easily crossed. The Osage Indian, Skiatooka, was a frequent trader at the post so it has been suggested that this may be the connection that resulted in the town's name. Historical records have conflicting data as to the origin of Skiatook's name. One story is that the town was founded on land that was the home of a prominent Osage Indian, Skiatooka, and the community around his home was called Skiatooka's Settlement. Another story is that the name was Cherokee in origin meaning either "big injun me" or describing a large man or a vast tract of land. The Skiatook Post office was establish at Rogers's store in the 1880s, and in 1892, the name was changed from Ski-a-took to its present form.

St. Gregory's College   A Catholic university in Shawnee, Oklahoma, founded by the Benedictine monks of St. Gregory's Abby in 1875. In 2000 it changed from a junior college to a baccalaureate-conferring university.

St. John Baptist De La Salle   The founder of the Christian Brothers, an order of men dedicated to Catholic education.

St. Thomas More Society   An organization of Catholic lawyers that encourages its members to live according the principles and ideals exemplified by St. Thomas More in their personal and professional lives, in order to promote and seek justice.

Schism   A breaking away from the Church.

Spiritual Formation   The growth and development of the whole person by an intentional focus on one's spiritual and interior life, interactions with others, and spiritual practices (prayer, study of scripture, fasting, simplicity, solitude, confession, and worship).

"The Remains of St. Peter"   Author: Prof. Margherita Guarducci, 1965

Uniate Eastern Rite Catholic Churches - communities of Eastern Christians within the Roman Catholic Church.   They retain their own distinctive spiritual, liturgical, and canonical traditions. Many of the Eastern Rite Churches permit their priests to marry. Uniate churches are distinct from both the Orthodox churches and the so-called Independent churches of the East, neither of which recognize papal primacy.

Vatican II   An ecumenical council of the Roman Catholic Church opened under Pope John XXIII in 1962 and closed under Pope Paul VI in 1965. The Council sought to bring the Church into the modern world and is best noted for the revision of most of the liturgy, the replacement of Latin with vernacular languages in rites and more open relationships with non-Catholic denominations.

Vatican Liaison   See Cardinal Bernard Law.

Venerable   Title permitted by the Church to be prefixed to the name of a candidate for beautification. Also appropriate as the title of some religious and superiors.

ABOUT THE AUTHOR

Mary Vincent Dally was born on a farm near Sheridan, Oregon. The family later moved to Port Orford, Oregon where she graduated from high school and attended Oregon State University. She married Father Peter Dally at St. Christopher Episcopal Church in Port Orford in 1957. The Dallys have four adult children and two grandchildren.